THERE ON YOUR WORST DAY

TRUE STORIES FROM THE BLUE LINE

ALAN MERRICK

Published by Life Sized Publishing

Oakville, Ontario, Canada

ISBN (Paperback): 978-1-997021-08-7

ISBN (Hardback): 978-1-997021-09-4

Dedicated to my friend and mentor, Ernie. Always encouraging, and always positive no matter what storms were brewing.

And also, to all first responders that serve and give their all. Making huge sacrifices sometimes without thanks.

EARLY PRAISE FOR THE BOOK

What stood out to me most about this book was its raw and honest portrayal of life as a police officer. It sheds light on the emotional roller coaster police officers face every single day—going from a traumatic call that may stay with them forever to responding moments later of a complaint about a neighbor throwing rocks. No matter the situation, they are expected to remain professional, composed, and ready for whatever comes next. That level of resilience and dedication is truly remarkable. I for one would not be able to do that.

Having been on the other end of the radio, I have a deep appreciation for the work these men and women do. This book offers an eye-opening look into the realities of policing and the challenges officers face both mentally and emotionally.

I highly recommend this book to everyone. Whether you're considering a career in law enforcement, looking to better yourself, or simply curious about what a day in the life of an officer is really like. This book is well worth your time. It's an insightful and compelling read that will leave you with a greater understanding and appreciation for those who serve their communities.

Karissa T. – 911 Dispatcher

I thoroughly enjoyed the stories in this book about getting the job and some of the interesting things seen on the job. I loved reading the first-hand accounts of things that most people could never imagine would happen. Reading the parts about individuals struggling with mental health issues is hard, but it is a reality of today's society.

Jon B. - Law Enforcement

There on Your Worst Day is captivating! It grabs your attention from the opening chapter and takes you down the different roads that law enforcement officers have to walk down daily. You see the process of someone coming to the decision of wanting to serve their community, and what they have to go through in order to get there. You get to see the ups and downs of different calls that police officers can be sent to, and at times the extreme trauma that they live through vicariously and the effect it can have on peoples lives.

The reason that There on Your Worst Day held my attention so well is because it is about a local central New York officer dealing with issues and problems that are not just organic to big cities like Chicago or Detroit. It really opens your eyes to the things that we may not see, know or even think would be happening in our small part of Central New York.

Jason K. - Law enforcement

Contents

A Prologue

I write this now in a much different environment from where I do my report typing. Currently in a seated position on my couch, I am comfortable and not weighed down with twenty pounds of gear. My laptop is straight in front of me as opposed to a car monitor that sits at the center of a police vehicle, forcing me to lean to my right to type. There is no urgency, no rush to document vital information. I can take my time to put down my thoughts, keeping my eyes on the screen without having to glance up and around every few seconds to check my surroundings like a bobblehead.

When I write reports in my patrol car in the dead of night, I must anticipate surprise interruptions. At home, the only thing I have to worry about is my cat bolting across my keyboard, which he is apt to do on occasion. But I have learned that even the most secluded spots with dark corners hide late-night wanderers who seemingly materialize out of nowhere when I am concentrating on my reports. I can only speak about my own experiences and the small city I work in when I say that people walk around all night long. But I can speak for every officer who has ever been startled by the face of a stranger outside their car window when they glance up from their screen when typing a report in an out-of-the-way spot on their grid – their beat – during a quiet moment between calls on the night shift. That is why we glance up and around as much as possible when we are writing. But now, in the comfort of my own home with no one to startle me but my cat, I can focus on the task at hand... writing about the funny, strange, and heartbreaking calls I've been on during my time as a police officer, weaving in stories from my days working at a local homeless shelter, and sharing my thoughts on addiction, mental illness, homelessness, and more.

INTRODUCTION

The collection of stories in *There on your Worst Day: True Stories from the Blue Line* is not written to elevate my experiences as a police officer above those of other officers. The true heroes in law enforcement, ambulance services, the fire service, the military, and countless other professions rarely receive recognition for the burdens they carry or the sacrifices they make every day. I have worked beside men and women whose courage, wisdom, and composure far exceed my own. Many of them could write stories far more dramatic than anything found in these pages. What I offer here is simply my perspective – one officer's attempt to make sense of the people, pain, humor, and humanity encountered between one call and the next.

Before becoming a police officer, I worked in a homeless shelter where I witnessed firsthand the complicated realities of mental illness, addiction, poverty, trauma, and broken family systems. Those years shaped the way I see people on the street, in crisis, and behind closed doors. They taught me that many of society's deepest problems do not exist independently of one another. Domestic violence, homelessness, substance abuse, untreated mental illness, neglect, and generational dysfunction are often tangled together in ways that are difficult to separate. Later, as a police officer, I encountered those same struggles again and again – not in statistics or headlines, but in living rooms, alleyways, emergency rooms, jail cells, abandoned houses, and heartfelt conversations at two in the morning.

This book is a collection of true stories from those encounters. Some are heartbreaking. Some are disturbing. Others are strange, darkly humorous, or nearly impossible to believe. Police work exposes a person to the extremes of human behavior: the violence people are capable of, but also the resilience they possess. Over the years, I have responded to scenes that still echo in my memory – parents grieving unimaginable loss, individuals destroyed by addiction, victims trapped in abusive homes, mothers desperate for help caring for their disabled adult children, and people battling mental illness with little support and nowhere to go. I have also encountered moments so bizarre and absurd that they could only happen in this line of work: domestic disputes involving mustard-covered husbands, strange midnight calls, people behaving in ways no academy could prepare you for, and incidents that still leave me shaking my head years later.

One experience that remains with me occurred during my sixth year on the job, when I received a "Courageous Officer of the Year" award. Truthfully, I never felt deserving of it. The recognition came after I transported a fire victim to the hospital in an ambulance during a tragic scene where two children lost their lives. The real heroes that day were the officers and firefighters who ran into a burning building trying to save them. What I remember most is not the award, but the sound of a mother's screams after learning her children were gone. Those are the moments first responders carry with them long after the lights stop flashing and the reports are filed away.

People often imagine police officers as unaffected by what they see. The reality is far more complicated. You cannot repeatedly witness trauma, chaos, violence, addiction, and despair without it leaving some kind of mark. Yet the job also teaches resilience. Officers learn to compartmentalize, to laugh when they can, and to keep moving because another call is always waiting. This book is not meant to glorify the profession or portray me as someone who has everything figured out. I have made mistakes throughout my career and will undoubtedly make more. Rather, these stories are an honest attempt to pull back the curtain on a profession most people only glimpse from the outside.

Some names, identifying details, and locations have been changed to protect privacy and show respect to those involved. Dialogue has been reconstructed as accurately as memory allows. While certain details may fade with time, the emotions behind these experiences do not.

More than anything, I hope these stories help readers better understand the world that many first responders step into every day and the societal problems that continue to grow in the shadows around us. I hope they encourage compassion for people who are suffering, respect for those who serve, and reflection on the systems that often fail the most vulnerable among us. If this book also helps my family and friends better understand why I sometimes think, speak, or see the world differently after years on the job, then it has served an even more personal purpose.

These stories are tragic, funny, unsettling, hopeful, frustrating, and at times unbelievable. But they are real.

This is not based on a true story.

This is a true story.

1

THE LONGEST DAY.....

The dirty knife was inches from my face. My eyes seemed to home in on that blade and the fresh blood on the handle (tunnel vision), the man who was holding the blade and everything else around me may as well not have existed. It was just me and this stranger in the dirt, fighting over the knife. The wrists of the young man were covered in blood. *Is it his blood? I know it's not mine*, I remember thinking. The knife went from hand to hand as I attempted to get a grip on his wrists, my own hands sliding off from the blood like a pipe covered in oil. The man yelled something to me... some sort of expletive. The whole incident lasted only a few seconds, but it felt as if half an hour had passed. I knew the man had stuck the knife into his own neck just as I had arrived on scene. What I was unclear about, however, was whether he was trying to stab himself again or stab me.

I thought about the body just next to us with the long brown hair. The tarp covering her was also covering her face. I couldn't tell if she was still alive, but it didn't look good. My main reason for trying to get the knife from this guy was to render the scene safe for paramedics to get in and possibly save her. If only I could get a grip on his wrists, I could hold his arms down. He was weak from loss of blood, yet he was still fighting with every last bit of energy he had. Was it jail or death that concerned him more? And to think, ten minutes ago I was just getting coffee and joking with Peggy, the nice woman who works at Stewart's, about it being a quiet morning.

The officer who arrived at the scene just moments before me witnessed the man jab the knife into his own throat. One last desperate attempt to escape whatever horrible crime he had committed. We more than likely had a homicide on our hands, but we're not about to let this man end things on his own terms. A failed attempt to kick the knife from his grasp on my part led to the current struggle I was in with the man on the ground. We were at a small clearing near the woods at the edge of a dead-end road.

The interesting thing about tunnel vision is that you believe you're entirely aware of what's going on, but are completely oblivious to what is transpiring around you. I never heard the other patrol units arrive behind me. Didn't hear or see them. I'm not even too sure how long I was struggling with this guy. All I remember was the extra hands coming from out of nowhere to help me grab the knife. And then she saved the day. A seasoned female officer who succeeded where I had failed, and kicked the knife out of his hand. The knife landed in the dirt yards away.

I thought it was over, but he jumped up and attempted to run for the knife. If he succeeded in getting the blade and came after one of us it would more than likely end a certain way. An officer never wishes to discharge their weapon. I grabbed at him before he could get far and only secured a grip on the back of his pants. I pulled hard and remember seeing him almost fall out of his pants as I upended him. He came down hard with a smack to the dirt floor a few feet from the knife. We were all on him, trying to get his hands behind his back. Someone hit him in the chest, probably in hopes of knocking the wind out of him. I could feel the blow of the strike as I was behind him and then felt blood splatter in the air. The guy rolled to his back, and I could see the large cut to his neck more clearly in the light. He had cut deep. Someone finally got handcuffs on this guy. I think it was me, but I'm not entirely sure. I just remember cleaning a lot of blood out of my cuffs the next day. The whole mess lasted only a minute, but was an entire blur.

An ambulance wasn't far. This was coincidentally one of the city's most popular events of the year. A race through the streets that brought in runners from around the world. More than 13,000 runners stacked back to back along one of the main roads at the edge of the city, all waiting behind the starting line, which was less than a mile from this grisly scene. Needless to say... All hands on deck that day.

The paramedics loaded the man into the ambulance and took off to the hospital. I was sure he wasn't going to make the trip there the way he was bleeding out. Another group of paramedics pronounced the girl on scene deceased. We didn't save anyone but the criminal, so it was not a proud moment. I stood up and then checked myself to make sure I wasn't cut. I had no injuries, but my arms and my uniform were covered in blood. Taking a moment to catch my breath, I took a better look at the environment I was in. It was an eerie scene. There had been a small fire going and music playing from a Bluetooth speaker. I remember thinking when I had just pulled up that it was someone's campsite out near the woods. That is, until Officer Basco drew his gun. Running out of my patrol vehicle, I left my radio in the car. Normally, it would be attached to me, but due to the large race and extra staff, all that was left was a radio with no corded mic.

The race had been halted moments before it was set to start due to this emergency less than a mile away. The runners at the starting line were probably all wondering what had happened. Fear was still pretty fresh from the Boston Marathon. I was also supposed to be at that starting line, ready to run as well. All roads nearby had been completely closed off, bar emergency responders.

After the crime scene tape went up around some trees and the scene was secure, I needed to get this blood off me. Investigators were now showing up as the small, dead-end street became packed with police vehicles. I walked to the nearest house, which was only a few yards away. A nice old woman was outside on her front lawn trying to discern the extent of the events that had just unfolded. The crime scene tape had portioned off a small bit of her front yard near some trees. The police vehicles that blocked her driveway, as well as her view of everything else, added to her confusion.

"Do you have a hose, miss?" I asked her politely, hoping not to scare her – I must have appeared ghastly in the state I was in. She was quiet for a moment, as if she didn't understand. "Like a garden hose?"

"Yes," she replied, "It's at the back of the house... You can use it." She could see I was covered in blood, but luckily didn't ask what it was from. What she said next threw me back a bit. "Will I be able to mow my lawn today?" I looked at her, not quite understanding what she had just asked me. Not "was everyone alright, are you okay?" She must have sensed my misunderstanding. "I planned to mow my lawn today. Will I be able to? You won't all be here all day, right?"

"No, miss, you can mow your lawn this afternoon." She had no clue about the evil that had occurred just yards from her front door. It was lawn mowing day, and that needed to get done. I washed off the now sticky blood as best as I could; the uniform would have to wait. The warm July sun was now peaking over the trees as the temperature continued to rise. I felt like I was still sticky all over from this mess. Exhaustion doesn't describe where I was at. I had been awake for almost two days, and sadly, this wasn't the worst part of my day. But to understand how I got here, we have to go back thirty-two hours.

It's 10:30 pm and my alarm sounds to tell me it's time to get up and ready for work. With not nearly enough sleep, I struggle out of bed in the hope that it's an easy night. A warm Friday night in July forecasts that it will not. Working as a patrol officer in a small city has its pros and cons. With about two years on the job, I'm no longer considered a rookie but still feel like I've barely grasped all of what the job entails. It's dynamic work that's always changing. You're always second-guessing yourself, making judgment calls on the fly, and you end up finding a balance between keeping your superiors happy and your peers. I was not a go-getter by any means, but I tried to do the best I could with what was put before me. As intelligent as I was, the job at times made me feel stupid. But at the very least, I was grateful for the job and the opportunity given to me. I proposed to handle one call at a time.

The events that occur on any given night can be overwhelming to someone less emotionally secure. You see the worst of what a city has to offer... people at their lowest doing awful things to each other, people that can't handle their emotions or booze. Sometimes, driving home from work, I'm amazed at all that I can witness in a night. All the conversations. All the same people committing the same crimes, without the desire to change their lives. This is just a small city and it's quite a thought when you realize how big the world is – cities filled with other people, all with the same issues. I got on scene to one call regarding a young man who was found unresponsive in his bed by a family member and had to inform the mother that her son is gone... then to a domestic where the woman's boyfriend threw bleach all over her clothes because she was out all night... then its straight to a mental health issue call for a guy who jumped out of a window and now has glass in his arm... then to a woman complaining because someone parked too close to her vehicle and she wants it moved right away – as she calls me names and says I just don't want to help her because I'm lazy and stupid. I started to enjoy doing absolutely nothing on my days off; I wanted no chaos and only peace.

A majority of the time on the night shift, we are dealing with someone, or multiple people, who are drunk, high and/or emotionally unstable. I've found it's beneficial to act like the calmest person in the world when I get there to try to tone the levels down. Body language conveys so much more than we do verbally. Some people, however, will not listen to sound reason, no matter what you attempt to convey to them.

I stop for coffee at the nearest gas station and get into work right on time, change into my uniform and sit in roll call. The hardest part of the midnight shift has always been getting out of bed. The midnight to 8 am shift isn't the most sought-after position for any job. But it has its perks. Most of the crazy parts of the night happen before 4:00 am...usually. This leaves a good amount of time to finish paperwork and catch up on other tasks. On busy nights, you can handle anything from three domestics to two motor vehicle accidents and any number of criminal mischiefs or suspicious activities. Alarms and abandoned calls were just a nuisance. A full night of calls and a morning of paperwork, I started to enjoy the times I would find myself racing the dawn to get everything tied up to be out on time.

It was the usual calls for the night. A domestic incident, a small fight, two noise complaints, two alarms, and one stray husky. Starting the job was a sort of culture shock for me; it was eye-opening to see how other people lived and acted around each other. The rudeness was one thing that caught me off guard. I must have been raised to be extremely polite; I always believed manners made the proper man. There is a lack of manners on these streets. One thing that threw me off was how people answered the door in the city. I had always known people to call out "Who is it?" or "Who's there?" What I had been greeted with was a rushed and almost angry "Who?" A plain and simple "Who?" I wasn't sure how to respond, so I said, "Uh, it's the police, sir. We're looking for Mr. Owl."

The clock on the dashboard of my patrol car hit 7:30 a.m. when I got the call. The day shift was short-staffed, and I had to stay until noon. It was going to be tight. I promised to be at my cousin's graduation party and now I have to go there right after work. I worked through the next four hours and waited for the noon bell to toll. When 11:30 a.m. came around, someone called in because she found a stray dog. It was another hour before I got the dog up to our local shelter and completed the two pages of paperwork for a stray dog intake. Then I was out.

I went home to change. It was hot and sunny by now, and I enjoyed it as much as a slap to the face. A cool, dark room was what I wanted – AC kicking and hours of quiet sleep. But on I went to the grad party. Deciding to stay later than I had planned, I caught up with family I hadn't seen in a few years. It was always the same questions: "How's work going for you?" and "What have you been up to in your free time?" and "Do you still like working overnights?" The afternoon passed quickly, and at 4 p.m. I still had time to get home, make a quick dinner, pack my running clothes for the race after work, and sleep for a few hours.

But then I received a phone call and news I wasn't expecting. It was the unexpected loss of a close friend. It wasn't that I was devastated – we weren't best friends – it was just one of those friendships where you tell the other person you are going to make time to catch up, and you never do. You always say there is more time, until there is not. I felt as if I was in a state of shock as I hung up the phone. Not entirely sure how to feel, I started to just go through the motions of getting things ready for work tonight and the run tomorrow.

Sleep. You fickle beast. So far away from me at times. So hard to attain. It had been almost twenty-four hours since I'd last slept and I should be able to pass right out. I wanted to, I was exhausted. But sleep eluded me. I really only had about four hours left until I had to be at work, and I couldn't sleep as much as I tried. I knew it was time to throw in the towel; I was not getting any sleep that night. I sat on my couch and counted the minutes down until work.

I prayed I could make it through the next eight hours of work, complete the run, and then sleep for a full day.

The coffee on my way to work didn't even begin to cut it. I would need a high-octane, double-caffeinated, sugary boost of energy. Over-caffeinated, sleep-deprived, and mentally shot, working is the last thing I should be doing. But this is the one night of the year that an officer doesn't call off. Everyone works this day for the biggest event in the city. All I could do was tell myself to get through the shift, run my best race, and not have a heart attack doing it. But I debated with myself over whether I should call it now and not run. My old self was telling me that I still had it in me from when I was eighteen, but the other part of me had to remind myself that I was pushing thirty-five and I had never run a race that long on so little rest. Like most sane and intelligent men, I decided to just push through it all and if I dropped, I dropped.

Every minute was a struggle. I remember everything from that shift, as it was an uphill battle all the way. Back in the locker room, putting on the vest and duty belt, I decided there was no way I would be able to run the race in the morning. I was just too physically and mentally shot. The energy drink was doing nothing. But, I told myself, at least I could bank on getting out of work on time. After all, work had just held me over yesterday morning because they were short-staffed. They couldn't hold me over again... right? Over the years, I had gotten used to the lack of sleep with the shift and was testing different diets and supplements to see if I could cheat rest. There is no substitute for sleep, at least not yet. This was a different type of exhaustion, though. After almost three years on the job, I had yet to use a sick day and I planned to keep it that way as long as I could. The stubbornness in me was going to kill me first. All I had to do was keep telling myself that the night would be over shortly... just get through – one minute at a time.

Years prior, our cross-country coach had drilled into us one simple rule – the mind quits before the body. I didn't even want to run as a sport. Who likes running? But I joined the team my freshman year because my best friend, Jack, said it would be fun. As far as I know, that is the only time he's ever lied to me. Eight or more miles a day on average was the typical cross-country practice. And when we weren't doing distance, we were running hills – our school was surrounded by steep hills. Our amazing coach and all those hills were the reason why we won two state titles. We were trained to never quit and to push harder when things got tough. In my first year of cross-country, I was not one of the better runners, even though my coach told me I had the ability in me and just wasn't trying hard enough. I assured him I was giving my all. Yet I wasn't. One race at the end of the season, I really opened myself up and crossed the finish line in fourth place. After that, I didn't train with the junior varsity boys. I was on varsity, and that's the last thing I wanted to happen. From there, I just continued to get better. And that's when I realized that I had no idea of my abilities. We are all capable of so much more. It was time to stop thinking about what I couldn't do and just tell myself I could. I've applied that into every area of my life... and it's given me a lot of extra work to do. Now, at work, all I had to do was just shut my brain off and get through one minute at a time.

The brain is the most powerful machine known in the universe. In the middle lies the Anterior Mid-Cingulate Cortex, a region of the brain responsible for willpower and drive. The interesting thing about this part of the brain is that it can expand the more a person pushes themselves through undesirable circumstances. The ultimate flex.

Right off the bat, as soon as I secured my patrol car, a domestic dropped in my zone. This poor woman probably just wanted a quiet night, as I did. She unfortunately chose a partner who was prone to jealousy and rage. I arrived on the scene to find all of the windows in her apartment busted out by her ex-boyfriend, who was upset with her for God knows what. It was the most glass I had ever seen on someone's floors. The man had left before I got on the scene, as most do. I put on a friendly face for the poor woman and started the paperwork and photographs. Charges were signed but the offender hid well from us that night, so now he would have a warrant hanging over his head.

The rest of the night consisted of a small fight, a missing person's report, and a domestic dispute right around 4 a.m. I was finally able to park my car in the lot of a pizzeria at 4:45 a.m. to start my paperwork. Less than four hours to go… I knew I could make it. I stopped at my apartment after my paperwork was completed to get a bottled water. As I walked back to my door to leave, I glanced briefly at my bed in my room like it was a long-lost friend. I imagined how amazing it would be to just lie down for a minute and rest my eyes. But I decided not to tempt fate, walked out the door, and promised myself that I would come straight home to sleep in three hours.

The sound of the engine humming low and steady was the only sound that could be heard in that dark corner of the parking lot before sunup. I sat parked near the rear of the unoccupied lot of the park below some low-hanging branches of some trees. The only thing shining light around me was the computer screen monitor and the car's dashboard. Other than that, the entire parking lot and park were completely dark. My thoughts were on nothing. My mind was clear for the first time in a long time, as I sat entirely still, staring straight ahead into the darkness. But it wasn't out of a calm resolve; it was more out of a severe lack of energy. I couldn't find any thoughts to hold; my brain wasn't working as it normally would. Like the hands of a clock that still spin, the gears are moving, but nothing's catching. I was beyond exhausted now, yet I was actually feeling alright. I don't know if it was pure focus or a type of resolve that had come over me, but I felt at peace... like things were going to be okay.

2

....CONTINUED

At 5:30 a.m., I got the call that I was dreading. It was Sergeant Lafleur, and he was not calling to ask how my night was going.

"Merrick, I know you were held over yesterday, and I'd hate to ask, buddy, but we had a call in for the day shift. I really need someone just to help out." Sergeant Lafleur was the type of guy who was so friendly, you couldn't say no. This would help me not feel guilty about skipping the race, I figured. "I can't make you stay after," he continues, "but if you do, it would be a huge help."

"Yeah, I can, Sarge," I remember my mouth saying the words, but I heard screaming coming from somewhere. It was only a few moments before I realized it was my brain.

"Thanks, pal," he replied. "I'll just have you in a spare car to go anywhere around the race course, wherever you're needed, and we can have you out by 10 a.m. at the latest."

Okay, so I'll be out of work four hours from now instead of two. What's two extra hours? I thought. I didn't know at that time, however, that I would not be off at 10 a.m. An evil was brewing miles away that I was completely unaware of... a domestic of the worst kind. And I'd be face-to-face with that mentally unhinged dark individual soon. It would be about twelve more hours before I finally made it home.

The sun had fully risen over the horizon, and it was truly a perfect day for a race. Parking my patrol car at the station, I was given an unmarked patrol vehicle that was at least equipped with a light bar and siren, but not much else. We were also short one radio since pretty much everyone who works for the department was working the event. So, I was given a radio with no corded microphone. I had to keep the damn thing on the seat next to me. I felt like I was driving my grandfather's car with no separated front seat or armrest. It was 7 a.m. and I went from spot to spot on the course helping move barricades, obviously after stopping to get a hot coffee and something to snack on.

All of a sudden, I was flagged down by Sergeant Coswell. An out-of-state runner was dropped off near the finish line instead of the starting line. Now, a majority of the time, we would just say, "Tough luck. We can't just taxi every runner around due to a minor mistake." But this was a high-profile runner, and it was imperative he start the race on time.

"Merrick!" Sergeant Coswell calls out from the middle of the street in the midst of a group of runners. She had been placing barricades along the course with everyone else.

"Yes, ma'am?"

"Get this man to the starting line. Quick as you can," She advised me after she walked the runner over, that he was one of the elite runners. His ride dropped him off and left and there were no shuttles from our location to the start.

There's no time to catch the guy's name, but I let him sit up front, moving my radio to the center of the seat. I just looked at him and said, "Buckle up," as we flew down the street like I was attempting to hit 88 mph and save a clock tower (Not going over 50 and obeying all traffic lights). Now I'm not gonna lie. This was the most fun I've had in quite a while. The roads were bare of traffic as most streets were closed down and I got to drive this runner without hindrance to the race starting line. I felt like Elaine on *Se-*

infeld trying to get her friend to the airport on time. The runner was having fun; I could tell by the way he held the *Oh shit handle* and smiled.

"How's your day going?" he politely asks as we carefully cross an intersection before I slam back on the gas.

Do you really want to know? Do you want me to start from the lack of sleep, the emotional distress I'm in due to losing a friend, or the exhausted state I'm operating under? "It's going good, just passing the time," I replied instead.

"Perfect day. Hope you don't have to work too much longer."

"I was supposed to run this race," I shouted to him over the noise of the loud wind coming in from my window. I could have told him my running ability, which would have been a surprise, but I didn't have the energy to keep up the conversation. Plus, we were nearing our destination.

"Oh, really?" he wasn't concerned.

"Yeah, but I'm working the overtime." We arrived at the starting line in time. I wished him good luck and started back towards downtown, counting the hours until I could leave.

The calls came in as background noise from the radio on my seat. There's always some issue, some emergency coming from dispatch. A lot of the "emergency" calls are exaggerations. It comes down to people making a big issue over little things, people making a big issue just to get the cops there, or people making a big issue because they don't have all the facts. Once in a while, you get a real emergency... something legitimate. Usually, you can tell. It's a feeling in your gut. But today, I was emotionally and mentally disconnected and couldn't hear what my gut was telling me.

I got one more small coffee from the Stewart's shop on the west side after I dropped off the runner. Why I had travelled all the way back in the opposite direction of the starting line was beyond me. Dispatch was advising of more calls coming in regarding their original call, something at the large park on the east side. The dispatcher sounded slightly distressed. "Man injured a female in the park." "Welfare check on Wilson Court." Apparently, calls had come in from out of state of a man killing a female. All officers had their assigned posts to the race, and the day shift wasn't going to take over for another few minutes. There were few patrol units available, and this was what my car assignment was for: to handle anything that popped up. One officer was already close by and was responding. I was on the other side of the city, but I was going to make my best time. The window was down and a nice breeze came in as I went close to seventy on Ashland Street towards Wilson Court. This was hopefully a prank call, and I could get back to my coffee and cruising around. But the dispatchers continued to relay information, and you could hear panic in their voices. They believed something was very wrong.

As I got to Wilson Court, a nice old man (a volunteer) had it blocked off with a barricade. The race was set to go off five hundred yards away in twenty minutes. The poor guy had no idea what was going on and refused to move. I had to flash my lights to show him who I was, as my car was unmarked. He smiled and moved the barricades. I heard him say something as I drove by, as if he was trying to make small talk.

I've lived in this city my whole life. I've been patrolling it for only two years, but have been down all but a few streets. This was one of them – a small, dead-end road of nice, little, quaint houses that ends in a clearing in the woods for no reason. I saw Officer Basco's patrol car up ahead and could smell smoke from a fire. It looked like someone was camping out and I remember thinking *oh man, what a weird place to camp...* That's when I saw Basco pull his gun out from his holster and point it towards something.

I jumped out of my car as soon as it was in park, leaving the radio. I caught up to Basco.

"He just stabbed himself in the neck," Basco announced. He stepped behind me and started to call out the situation to dispatch and anyone else who could respond immediately. *Holy shit*, I thought, as I pulled my gun out and aimed at the man. I saw the guy, lying there as if he was taking a nap, hands on his chest, knife in his hand. He was a younger man with brown hair. I couldn't recall more because I was entirely focused on the knife. He wasn't moving. That's when I noticed the brown hair near him under a tarp. He had laid his head on the tarp – apparently the other person's stomach. I assumed it was a female.

She wasn't moving either. Basco called paramedics and I knew they wouldn't be able to get in to help this girl until that knife was out of this guy's hands and he was detained. Basco had said the guy stabbed himself in the neck and I could see a lot of blood, but I couldn't be sure of whose blood it was. I decided to take a chance. The guy seemed to be losing consciousness – if he hadn't already – and I was sure I could kick the knife out of his hands. Some eerie music was playing the whole time from a Bluetooth speaker. Things seemed to slow down as I approached the guy with my gun still drawn.

I never played football, but I was pretty confident I could kick the knife out of his hands. He seemed like he was almost dead. I was only a foot away now. Just as I swung one foot back and prepared to kick hard, he opened his eyes and looked at me. It was as if he were playing possum the whole time. His eyes fixed on me, and I saw his muscles tense as he gripped the blade tightly. I kicked... and missed. The next moment, I holstered my weapon because I needed both hands to try to grab the knife from him. I was on the ground over him, but I just couldn't get a grip. And this gets us caught up to where we left off.

I thanked Miss "I-need-to-mow-my-lawn-today" for her garden hose usage and I went back to work. The captain walked my way as I returned to the scene, and he could see the blood on my uniform.

"How are you doing?" he asked sincerely.

Do you really want to know? "Good, just a little tired," I replied.

"Did any blood get in your mouth or your eyes or anything?"

"I don't think so," I said as I checked myself over. A week ago, I was bitten by something, probably a spider, which left three scabs on my left hand. During the scuffle, they had opened up. I showed the captain the marks on my hand.

"You should probably go to the hospital for decontamination with Mike, just for precaution," The captain suggested. Mike had gotten blood in his mouth while we were on the ground wrestling with this guy.

It was midday when we got back to the station to start paperwork after decontamination at the hospital. I was running on some kind of reserve fumes. I don't know where energy comes from, but I'd like to. The reports were completed after an hour or so, and I got in my car to leave work. Part of me did not want to go home, to be alone at my apartment after all of this, even though sleep was what I needed. I desired to be around regular people, to have some semblance of normalcy. I decided, however, that that was probably not the best idea in my disheveled condition and made the short drive home.

I finally washed up completely. In the comfort of my own shower, I could fully see all the places I had missed at the hospital. It is a surreal experience to wash away someone else's blood. I'm not saying I went through the worst thing that can happen to an officer on the job. Every day, officers around the country experience horrific, heartbreaking, unthinkable things, yet many people don't recognize that. It is too easy, especially these days, to assume that most police officers are the bad guys. Every cop I know would do anything to help someone in danger. Even a stranger. And even if it means putting themselves in a life-or-death situation.

Once I had time to decompress from the day's events, my thoughts dwelt on the victim of the stabbing. I could never imagine what those parents of that poor girl had to deal with that day and what they would have to go through in the coming days. My heart truly hurt for them.

The struggle with her killer sent adrenaline running through my body when I was already at a point of physical and mental exhaustion. It changed my brain chemistry. I look for ways to push myself to the limits and I want to continuously build my endurance. My work keeps my mind and body active, but it also has a way of draining my emotional energy. I needed sleep, but I also needed mental rest. I needed to break entirely before I could rebuild.

I slept close to fourteen hours that night. It had been years since I slept that long. For a moment, my thoughts were foggy. The circumstances surrounding the stabbing were rather fuzzy. *Was it just a dream?* I remember thinking to myself when I awoke. No, it really happened.

But I felt... a greater resolve. More than that... I felt a desire to do more. My mind wasn't quite working the same way and I could feel it. The stress and anxiety were gone, and I felt as if I were born anew.

Stress is an interesting thing. It can't be avoided – humans experience stress as an adaptive survival response – but stress can either save us or tear us down. Explaining this paradox can be difficult, but let me try. When the brain perceives a threat – either a physical threat or some sort of unknown danger – it tips over the starting domino that leads to a chain reaction of involuntary chemical responses in the body. Stress hormones, like adrenaline and cortisol, flood the body to prep it for a 'fight or flight'. The heart rate increases, energy levels spike, the mind sharpens, breathing becomes shallower ... all ways our bodies gear up to fight off a threat or run away from it. When it works like this, stress is a good thing. It is a line of defense... protection from danger.

However, when stress becomes chronic, sustained elevations in cortisol and other neurochemicals can alter brain chemistry and function. Prolonged stress exposure can disrupt the parts of the brain that control memory, mood, concentration, and decision-making. Over time, these chemical shifts can contribute to difficulties with concentration, emotional regulation, and vulnerability to anxiety or depression.

For me, however, my relationship with stress changed after this incident. It is not easy to describe it. Do you remember the 1999 movie, *Office Space*? In it, the main character is hypnotized and wakes up with a new 'don't sweat the small stuff' attitude. I sort of felt like that. Everyday stress and anxiety no longer bothered me. Somehow, I was able to let it go – without hypnosis!

Don't get me wrong... I still made plenty of mistakes after this point in my life, but the fear and stress seemed to be gone. There were no longer any worries about anything because worrying was a waste of time. I had forgiven everyone for anything they had done to me because grudges were a waste of time. Spending any time on grudges or being upset at people for the way they act or do things was a waste of energy.

I later learned that, like PTSD, severe stress could impact the brain in one of two main ways. Severe stress can damage a mind and create negative symptoms, or it can strengthen and rebuild it. In my case, the severe stress didn't come from just the stabbing incident; it came from a mix of everything leading up to it, including lack of sleep. The tussle with the knife triggered my body's fight or flight response and the surge of adrenaline was the catalyst to my brain forming new neural connections. I lucked out in the way this manifested in me. With this newfound 'chill' attitude, I started to look at things more inquisitively.

A few days later, I received a call from a daytime sergeant that threw me off. At first, I thought maybe there was an emergency at work.

"Merrick, how are you holding up?" he asked.

"Great," I said. In that moment, I realized I had responded too quickly and probably sounded insincere. It was foolish of me because I knew he was calling to check in with me after the traumatizing incident. He was just doing his job. *Call the family members and friends of the poor girl who lost her life, not me,* I thought.

To truly understand the life of a police officer, these experiences need to be shared and discussed. Most of the time, we are interacting with people on one of the worst days of their lives. Everyone has moments of chaos, catastrophe, and confusion. Some people seem to get more of them than others. No one likes it when their roller coaster plummets to the lowest point on the track, but I've learned that these rock-bottom moments are necessary. Growth comes from discomfort. An easy life is not practical, nor is it promised. We learn more from our failures than we ever could from our successes. Looking back, I can see that the pivotal moments of my life came on days when I was thrown into a storm, faced the unknown, or was forced to take a big risk. On those days, I learned more about myself, what I was capable of, and how to overcome the obstacles in my path.

My personal growth over the past few years has been tremendous, and I can only imagine what life lessons are still to come. I am not wishing misery on anyone, but from time to time, I hope you have the wind at your front and sun at your back... because you're not going to be your best you, without going through the worst.

3

Bad Boys

"Who has the keys?"

The state trooper was already extremely irritated with us, I could tell. We had been parked in an empty parking lot of a restaurant a few miles from where we caused the current issue that brought this trooper our way. I guess it wasn't really smart to remain in town after the stunt we had just pulled. There were at least five other police units there and we had been having just a grand time for the past half an hour, laughing about what we had done. "I'll ask again..." the trooper continued – he was pissed. "Who has the keys?" The truth was, none of us knew who had the keys. As far as I knew, we left them back with the steamroller where we had parked it, in that jerk's driveway.

I was twenty-one, I believe, at the time. There was heavy road construction going on towards the south end of town where the village met the highway. They were expanding the road by another two lanes, and some big construction company, that we didn't know was locally owned, had picked up the contract. I was young, but old enough to know you don't leave the keys in your most expensive piece of equipment when you leave for the day.

It was the largest steamroller I had ever seen. I had yet to see one larger – two giant drums on either end and a platform to stand on. There was enough room for the three of us to stand and steer the large wheel at the same time. We were ecstatic when we found the keys in the damn thing. After a few minutes of some loud noises coming from the engine as we tried to start it up, I gave up and started walking away. My two friends were resolved, however, and got the machine started and moving forward. I turned around in a state of panic and wonder as I saw this thing barreling down the road. Running as fast as my feet could carry me, I caught up and Jack lifted me up onto the platform again.

The steamroller was honestly so loud, I have no idea why it took the neighbors so long to call the cops. We ran over two stop signs, flattened them out like hot butter over toast into the road. Part of me panicked because I was sure that Matthew wanted to drive the steamroller through a house. We figured out how to stop the thing and parked it in some guy's driveway that we knew to be a local hot head, a business owner of a restaurant that likes to get snappy with his customers and staff. The last thing I remembered was running back to the car and leaving the area before the police showed up. I had no clue someone took the keys to the steamroller. And we probably would have gotten away with it if I weren't still wearing the hard hat when the state trooper passed us by.

"Matthew must have the keys," I said to the cops and my friends all at once. Matt had left the gathering right after we had taken the steamroller for a ride. He had to get up for work early in the morning. Coincidentally, he had moved out of his house a month prior after a dispute with his parents and was currently sleeping in my mom's basement.

It was a quick ride in the back of the cop car to my mom's house. I was more concerned with what she was going to do than with any legal ramifications I could be facing. I knew I was technically an adult now, but I could still imagine the feel of a strike from a wooden spoon on my ass every time I start to make pasta sauce. The time she broke the spoon and I laughed... Oh, that was a mistake. Still, this wasn't the first time I sat in the back of a cop car. I was always getting in trouble. I've run from the cops numerous times as a teenager and my antics around town got me noticed by the authorities. I was hoping this would be the last time.

We woke up Matt, who had already passed out on his makeshift bed in the basement and found the key had, indeed, been stashed in his pocket. "Why did you take the key?" I shouted to him. But he had no clue he even took it – it was just a muscle memory habit when he turns an engine off, I guess. The cops were surprisingly cool about it, however. After they pounded on the door and woke my mother up, one of the officers simply couldn't hold back his laughter. The other one was trying hard to hold in a smirk. "Your son and his friends took a steamroller for a joyride, miss," he explained to my mom. I could see her confusion turn into amusement. She may have thought our little prank was funny, but she still yelled at Matthew and me when the police left.

We had our day in court. The judge ordered us to remain apart; he didn't want us to cause any more trouble together. Of course, we broke his order. The judge himself saw us hanging out in front of my house when he drove by – it's a small town.

When the next court date arrived, the judge said we would all go to jail right then unless we came up with bail money. I think it was like $1500. Until that moment, Jack had successfully kept this whole incident secret from his parents until that moment, but they lived right across the street and Jack needed bail money. He made the phone call, and we watched as Jack's parents marched across the street and up the lawn to the courthouse.

All in all, we were sentenced to community service and fifteen days of house arrest. That was a breeze. I had friends over and we ordered pizza. I had had some close calls in my youth, but the steamroller incident was the first and last time I was arrested.

I saw the trooper who arrested us a few years later; he remembered us and the steamroller incident. "How could I forget that?" he said, laughing. He shared with me that it was his first month as a trooper. He had just come from overseas, where they see real problems like gunfire every day, and his field training officer was pressing him to charge us with everything they could. In his eyes, we were just some young guys who took things a little too far... we didn't hurt anyone or damage anything. *Didn't they see the flattened stop signs?* I thought to myself. A few years into my career as a police officer, I got to work alongside him for a joint task effort with the state police. It was a weird, full-circle moment.

I shared this story for a reason. Most people see the more mature, well-mannered, friendly version of me when we meet. They have no clue how much trouble I caused back in my younger days. They think because I'm a police officer that I never ran from the cops. They assume I always followed the straight and narrow. They don't know about the younger version of me that broke into my school with my friend, Luke, and called the local police from the principal's office. We wanted them to know that we got that far into the building. Looking back at it now, I feel bad... I've had to respond to some of those similar calls. We didn't think about the consequences of our acts of rebellion. If we had caused someone to get into an accident on their way to that school, for example, that would have been our fault. At the time, however, we thought it was all harmless fun. I never wished ill will on anyone.

Yes, we were rambunctious, but we didn't hurt anyone, and we didn't destroy anything. Ironically, someone else broke into the school soon after I did and trashed the cafeteria. Since I had been boasting about my nighttime adventures in the principal's office, word spread that I did the damage. Within a week, I was in an investigator's office being grilled about the incident. He said they had fingerprints on the window from the fourth-floor hallway and I started to panic. *Oh shit, that's the window we used to get in.* I don't know if they ever found out who caused the damage, but it definitely was not me. Cameras went up in the school right after that.

A small, but significant shift in my mindset occurred a few months later. I was walking home from a friend's house and saw a local police vehicle park in front of my house. The paranoid part of me panicked. I thought I was caught... for what, I didn't know. It could have been any number of things that I had done in the past few years. The officer got out of his car and shined his light around the side of the house. I didn't recognize this officer (and I was familiar with all of them). He looked brand new. "Hey, is this your house?" he asked when he saw me walking toward the fence by the driveway.

"Yeah, it's my mom's house," I replied. "Is everything alright?"

"Someone called about a guy sneaking around the area, looking into cars. I saw some guy bolt past the side of your house when I pulled around the corner."

"Do you think he's hiding out near the back?" I ask. "It's all fenced back there."

"I don't know." The cop peered around as if hoping to catch a glimpse of the man. "I'm going to head around this side of the house and see if he's still back there."

"I can go around the other side, in case he tries to run around." As I spoke, I had a feeling he didn't want me to help out. I was surprised when he agreed. We took opposite sides of the house and met at the back. I was actually hoping this guy was going to come charging my way so I could tackle him and be a hero, but he must have jumped the fence before we got to the back. The cop shook my hand and thanked me for the help. This was the first positive interaction I'd ever had with a cop. I felt a bit of pride walking in through the front door and taking off my shoes. I was happy that I was there to help, but I didn't want to just be me anymore. I wanted to be him.

Many years later, when I was working at the Rescue Mission, I got a phone call from a close friend from my old college. I had kept in touch with my friend, Jonathan, and his family ever since I left college to move back home, taking trips at least twice a year to visit them. They had become like a second family to me. His Aunt Betsye and her husband, Ron, jokingly called me the son they never had, and referred to me as a brother to Jonathan and his sister, Allie. It was Allie on the other end of the phone that day. She didn't sound like herself; she sounded like she was in shock. Jonathan was dead, she told me. Shot and killed in his apartment. I couldn't believe it! Jonathan was the nicest guy I had ever met. I had never heard him say one negative thing about anyone. Who would want to kill him? There must be a mistake.

Allie told me how Jonathan had been helping a girl get back on her feet after leaving an abusive relationship. The jealous ex-boyfriend followed Jon to his apartment, got in through his front door, and shot him to death... then he turned the gun on himself.

I didn't know what to say; I didn't even know how I felt. That was the first friend I had lost at such a young age. Allie was definitely in shock. I was amazed she was able to maintain a conversation on the phone with me. Naturally, I took time off to go to the funeral. I kept expecting Jonathan to come out from the next room with a wisecrack grin on his face. It didn't feel real.

I stayed the night with Jonathan's family after the funeral and woke the next morning with a new determination. I said my goodbyes to my second family and started the drive back home, planning the whole way how I was going to get in shape and take any steps needed to become a police officer. I knew I couldn't turn back time. I knew I couldn't right the wrongs, but at least I could do my part to help prevent things like this from happening. Even if all it meant was being in the right place at the right time.

Less than a year later, I signed up to take the next police officer exam that was scheduled for the fall. Becoming a police officer, I learned, was a waiting game. Take the written test... wait a few months... take the agility test... wait some more... fill out a background investigation packet ... wait for the background check to clear... meet with the investigator... wait for an interview.

The first interview lasted more than an hour. I was definitely not prepared for it. Several men in suits or uniforms sat around a long table and all questioned me about everything I had ever done in life. I don't blame them; they need to know who each candidate is, how they deal with the public, and who can be trusted to carry a gun. The whole interview process had a very serious tone, at least for the first forty-five minutes. And then someone asked, “So... What about this whole incident with a steamroller?” It was quiet for a moment, and then everyone around the table burst into laughter.

4

A Mental Health Issue

The man was seated in the back of my patrol vehicle, handcuffed, and raving about everything from French fries to government conspiracies. To his credit, he knew the date was April 1st and kept saying April Fools. I had been waiting for my partner to finish the paperwork and get the charges signed so we could bring this man into the station and get him booked. We had arrived minutes prior after receiving a call from a scared social worker who had locked herself in her car from the crazed man who was threatening her. This poor woman went out for a smoke break from her job and had to run to her vehicle, which was closer than the back door of her work, to get away from this stranger who was screaming at her. The man had broken her passenger's side window before she dialed 911, he then proceeded to smear his feces on her remaining windows before we got there. I didn't see the feces on his arms and hands until after I had been touching him to get him in the back of my car. Fortunately, I was wearing gloves, unfortunately they were my nice gloves.

"What's your name, man?" I tried getting him to focus on talking to me before he got out of control in the back-seat. The last thing I needed was more mess to clean up.

"Joseph Allen," he replied without hesitation.

"Oh, what a coincidence. My name's Alan. So, we have that in common".

"I smeared that turd on that girl's windows; you can see my turd right over there," He said.

"I coincidentally haven't smeared any turds on anyone's windows," I replied. "So, I guess we don't have that much in common".

Charges were signed for the woman's damaged vehicle and the man was brought to the station. I proceeded to disinfect my backseat and wipe everything down, then washed my hands thoroughly and threw my gloves away. Hopefully, I won't need any for the remainder of the morning.

One of the biggest problems on the streets today is the battle with mental health issues. I don't think that's a big surprise to the public. But it is a problem that makes every other problem worse. In the small city where I work, there are numerous programs and services designed to help people struggling with a mental health issue, but how do you get someone the help they need when they don't want it?

Most mental health issues begin to surface at a young age, with or without the inclusion of drug use (but it's usually with). In my seven years of working with the homeless and addicted followed by my ten years on patrol, I have gotten to know a lot of the same people and witnessed their mental declines over the years. It is surprising how fast someone with a mental health issue can deteriorate even without a strong addiction issue.

The night had just started when my friend, Ivan, and I were sent to a call with very little information. The man on the other end of the phone did not speak English, so our dispatchers didn't have much to go on. They dispatched us to check on the man at his address on the east side of the city. Ivan and I arrived at the same time and parked our cars. I had made some good friends on this shift, but Ivan was a cut above the rest. He was the most relaxed and seemingly carefree person I had ever met. If I had met him anywhere else in life, I wouldn't have believed he was a cop. Just the way he talked and acted would make you think he smoked pot his whole life. Maybe it was just the night shift, but he always talked with his eyes half open and was apt to joke around more than be serious. When it came time to work, however, he took action, but he had a way with people that put them at ease. I was trying to adopt this skill myself.

We knocked on the front door of the duplex and a small, elderly man opened the door with a kind smile. We assumed he was our caller. The dispatchers were correct; he spoke no English. The man led us into the living room, which looked like a bedroom... it only had a mattress on the floor in the corner. There was no other furniture in the house. The only other thing in the room – besides the mattress, Ivan, the elderly man, and me – was a short man with shoulder-length hair. He was standing in the center of the room with his pants down around his ankles and his hands in front of his crotch. Wait a minute, no, he was holding it with what seemed to be a very strong grip.

"What's the problem?" Ivan said to the elderly man, as if there wasn't a guy standing next to us holding his penis. All the elderly man could do was point. I figured maybe this was his son and the guy had some mental issues.

"Are you okay, sir? Do you speak English?" Ivan then asked the man. No answer. The man clearly wasn't speaking to us and hadn't moved from his spot. He just stood there staring towards the door, squeezing his penis. He had such a grip on that thing I thought maybe it owed him money.

Ivan and I tried to pull his arms in separate directions to get him to let go, but he had the full vice grip. I could tell by the tense muscles in his arms that he was squeezing as hard as he could. We then tried to get the man's pants up, but we couldn't get them over his hands. "Why don't you just let go of your penis, man?" Ivan asked, as if the man didn't think of that. No reply. "Come on, man," Ivan continued, "Just let go of it."

Ivan called for paramedics because ultimately, we were going to have to transport the man to the hospital, whether for mental health reasons or medical reasons. The man refused to move and refused to walk. Luckily, he was about a foot shorter than us and not that heavy. Ivan took one side, and I took the other and we lifted him up like a scene from *Weekend at Bernie's* and moved him from the living room to the hallway and out the front door. The trip down the front steps was comical. We had him lifted in the air about six inches off the ground. We walked down the steps with him; he was as stiff as a board. That's when the paramedics pulled up.

"What's wrong with him?" the one guy asked. The man still had a death grip on his genitals. It was easier to see in the light of the streetlamp – it was wrapped around one hand like a clown getting ready to make a balloon animal.

"Just look at him," Ivan said. "He's got to be in pain."

"Did he say he was in pain?" the other paramedic asked.

"He doesn't speak English, and I don't think he wants to talk," I replied. "He has to go up to the hospital for a mental evaluation either way."

"Okay, let's get him in then." The paramedics helped us move the man up into the ambulance and onto the stretcher. I didn't go along with them to the hospital, but I heard about what happened. All of the doctors and nurses who were in that wing attempted to pull the man's hands from his penis. The attempts failed. They eventually sedated the man. Once he was asleep, his grip loosened, but the doctors never got the man to talk about his strange actions that night. To this day, I still don't know what caused the man to squeeze that hard. We never saw the man again. More than likely, he got the help he needed, at least one can only hope.

Homicide. Apartment complex in the northern part of the city. A woman went crazy and became violent with her own mother. She stabbed her multiple times with a pair of scissors and apparently tried to cut out her eyeballs. This was the first homicide of my career. I was stuck in that apartment with my partner, holding the scene down for our crime scene investigators to come back with some more equipment. The poor mother was upstairs, dead. I took a gander in the refrigerator and noticed five jugs of milk. Five. I remember thinking that it was odd... way too much milk to have on hand.

A year later, I was on my first scene of an infant death, the saddest call a police officer can get. The mother did not seem as concerned as I was, which I made a point of telling the medical examiner who was investigating the suspicious death. I was stuck in that house for way too many hours after the family was taken to the hospital. I took the pictures I needed to take and collected the evidence I needed to collect. All I had to do now was wait to be relieved so I could start my paperwork.

Alone in this filthy house, I didn't want to touch anything. Around five in the morning, I noticed something moving on the floor. I was in the kitchen trying not to accidentally lean on any walls, fighting the urge to sit in a chair. Standing for a long time wearing a duty belt can be uncomfortable for the hips. I looked closer at the floor and saw maggots crawling and wriggling about near my boots. I felt sick; I couldn't wait to get outside. The maggots appeared to be coming from underneath the fridge and I could smell what seemed to be rotting meat. Someone probably dropped some food, and it got lost under the refrigerator. I opened the fridge door to peer inside, almost afraid to look. It was filled with lots of nasty leftovers that were spoiled and gallons of milk that had gone bad.

On a quiet summer morning, I was sent to the nicer part of town for a reported burglary in progress. The guy who called stated that a person had broken into his house and was hiding under his bed. I arrived there anticipating a fight. This guy's pupils were about as large as pepperoni slices as he told me the intruder was still under his bed. He pointed toward the bedroom, an open door past his kitchen. Cautiously, I peeked in to find a small bed on a wooden frame, one inch off the floor. This was a point in my life when I did not believe in shape-shifters or one-inch-tall men, so I realized the caller was cracked out. I did not get a chance to check out his milk situation, but if I had to guess, chocolate. The man was known, however, for smoking synthetic marijuana. I was hopeful that this was his wake-up call, as I hadn't heard from him again.

Paranoia is one of the main symptoms we see with subjects who take synthetic drugs. It still amazes me that someone will willingly smoke synthetic narcotics, knowing full well that it is likely to put them in dangerous situations.

A few winters past I responded to a report of a male who jumped from a window at one of our local apartment complexes. I got to the scene first, just in time to see a man running across the street wildly and bleeding from his legs. I later came to find out that he had jumped through a third-floor window (luckily into a snow bank) because he believed someone was in his apartment trying to kill him. He was not willing to go to the hospital and despite our best efforts to assure him we only wanted to help him, it took three officers to get him restrained for his own safety and wellness.

Back on my grid, on another warm morning, the end of my shift was in sight. It was the hour when all my coworkers were hoping we had a smooth remaining stretch of the shift so we could leave on time. Unfortunately for me and my partner, Joe, it was not one of those mornings. We were sent to another duplex – this one in the more run-down part of the city – for a woman not acting quite right. Her family had called to say that she was barking and trying to bite them. We made our way there as the sun came up. One of the family members answered the door and led us to the kitchen. There, we found a heavy-set woman wearing only a long, colorful dress; I believe it is called a kanzu. She was lying on the floor, growling at her family and then at us. She crawled lazily over to my leg and for a moment, I thought she was going to bite my ankle; I shrugged her away and kept a distance. We motioned for her to stand up and speak with us, but she was paying as much heed as a house cat would.

When we turned to speak with her family, this woman – her family called her Amira – stood up, walked through the living room and to her bedroom, where she sat on the floor near the bed. We follow and continue trying to speak with her. Amira's family stated that this is unusual behavior for her. I would hope so.

Then someone mentions voodoo. *Wait... what?* I thought. Amira began making a noise ... something between growling and moaning. Joe and I both look at each other, knowing this would likely end in a trip to the hospital. When we tried to stand her up, Amira just batted our hands away. Then things went from strange to stranger.

Amira started vomiting this weird green slime into her hands and wiping it all over her body. All I could think at that time was that I was going to end up covered in that green slime, like a contestant on a Nickelodeon game show. And sure enough, after a long wrestle on the floor, I did. Amira wasn't going to the hospital willingly, and she put up quite a fight. Picture three adults sliding around on a hardwood floor slick with slime. I had slime on my sleeves and hands... I hoped the fire department would show up and turn the hose on me full blast.

I saw Amira a few times after that. One night, she was trying to ignite all the burners on a stove from a second-floor apartment. The man who called had apparently let Amira stay with him for a month, only to wake and find her trying to burn the house down. There was no food to cook in the house, only a fridge filled with... you guessed it... milk.

The last time I saw Amira was a few months ago. She was walking down one of the streets in my zone, smashing out people's windows with a piece of wood. What is going on? Didn't she get the help she needed? Isn't she getting ongoing help? Is our mental health system failing us? Sadly, it seemed she was not getting the help that she needed and her path was leading her towards further mental decline and arrests for preventable crimes.

It's these things that keep me up at night when I'm not working. Crime is one thing... and as much as I hate to admit it, crime makes some sense. People hurt other people out of anger. People destroy another person's property as retribution for some wrong done to them. People steal because they don't feel like paying, or they don't have the money to pay. People abuse drugs and alcohol because they can't control themselves or their addiction. It is wrong, but there is some logic behind such criminal behaviors.

But mental illness is not logical. It is sad. The number of people who are slowly falling into delirium and psychotic episodes seems to be growing year after year. At the same time, our society as a whole is becoming more aware of mental health issues. Some of the stigma surrounding mental health is slowly dissolving, and there are more programs, counseling centers, and avenues for help. Yet, the problem continues to grow. And there is no rhyme or reason for what they do, at least not to the observer. It is the individual's personal responsibility to keep up on their mental and physical health, but it's our responsibility as a whole to address these issues. And from what I have seen and experienced, we are failing in that responsibility.

Law enforcement officers, in my area and across the country, are increasingly encountering situations where untreated mental health issues intersect with other societal problems, like homelessness and addiction. This cocktail creates complex challenges that complicate what we are taught at the academy. When officers respond to calls involving individuals in crisis, they may find themselves acting not only as law enforcers but also as de facto social workers, crisis responders, counselors, and mediators. These encounters can require patience, specialized training, and time – resources that are often stretched thin in smaller or rural departments.

Mental health crises can also make these interactions with the police unpredictable, particularly when someone is confused, frightened, or unable to communicate clearly. Officers must balance the need to maintain public safety – and their own personal safety – with the responsibility to approach people in crisis with compassion and care. Without adequate community resources – such as crisis response teams, mental health services, and supportive housing – police officers may be left as the first and sometimes only point of contact for people in mental distress. This reality makes an already demanding job even more difficult. What is the answer? I don't know. But I do believe coordinated efforts between police, healthcare providers, and community organizations are needed to better address the root causes behind the mental health crisis.

I've encountered people who didn't deserve the hands they were dealt. People who are struggling to care for a family member without help. People who are clearly in over their heads.

Every time I pass a certain house in my community, I wonder how the woman who lives there is faring. I met her once when I was called to her home at 4:00 in the morning. She was wearing a helmet and knee pads and looked like she was ready for a round of roller derby. She seemed absolutely exhausted. Her sixteen-year-old daughter, a large girl, has a severe form of autism. She is nonverbal and prone to sudden, aggressive outbursts. She called 911 because her daughter had become so violent that she feared for her own safety.

Her daughter had been torturing her, she told me. She didn't have anyone to help her care for her daughter, and apparently, the girl was too far beyond the area of services offered locally. She expressed to me her desire to move anywhere in the country just to get her daughter into a long-term housing facility. It's not that she hated her daughter – I'm sure she loved her as any mother should – but she lived in terrible fear of her daughter. Every night, the poor woman slept on the couch or somewhere different to hide from her daughter and her fits of anger. If the daughter woke up and went to the mother's room to look for her, she often struck her on the head as hard as she could. She was no little girl – she was taller than me and much heavier. The mother's only recourse was to hide at night and sleep in different places – if she could sleep – all while wearing headgear to protect her. She stressed to me that she was worried her daughter would kill her one night... and I believed her. When I took down her birth date for the report, I did a double-take. I would have sworn the woman was at least fifteen years older than her actual age. She had only called a handful of times in the span of a few weeks and then the calls abruptly stopped. I had assumed one of the many programs she had written to had eventually reached out and was willing to help.

The issues I've highlighted in this chapter deal with the mental health issues concerning the public, but what about the first responders? The police officer who takes a toll after being a witness to difficult situations day in and day out? When I started to write these stories down, I did it mostly for myself and those close to me, so I would never forget them and have a collection of things to read when I retired. My plan was not to publish this originally. However, as I started to write more and more concerning nutrition, diet, and mental fortitude, I started to realize that maybe this could help someone and I felt it was an obligation to share these issues that are increasingly becoming a larger issue for first responders.

A police officer has to put up that tough exterior front both at work and at home; it's just how we are. I work with some of the toughest and most respectable fathers, mothers, leaders, team members, comedians, and counselors. And we all share the same job and the same stories. I don't imagine that other police departments are too different. But how are we reaching out to those friends/members when they are struggling internally and don't show it? Yes, there are plenty of programs and resources for those to reach out to when needed, peer support, as when that Sergeant called me after the major incident to check on how I was faring. But what about the issues that build over time? The constant barrage of domestics and emotionally disturbed calls, the officer dealing with issues all day long for other people, only to go home and not have the energy to deal with home issues. I truly can't speak for every department and only my own; they have a great collection of resources and there is always someone to talk to. But that is why I write this book, for the smaller departments, the less connected departments, the officers that don't know where to turn when things get overwhelming.

My law enforcement experience started ten years ago, but my experience in the mental health field started long before that. As I will go further into detail in the coming chapters, I worked as a residential aide at a homeless shelter and then became a supervisor for a rehabilitation program. This is where my fascination with mental health started. To see individuals struggling with the same issues and for the majority staying the same or getting worse. They all seemed to share one thing in common: past trauma. The workers in these fields continue on for those who do achieve victory over their addictions and illness. For the success stories, it's entirely worth it. Now I have to say, I am no nutritionist, dietician, psychologist, psychiatrist, doctor, or certified in any of these listed fields to treat or diagnose. But I can say that I have studied mental health and its relationship to trauma and nutrition for the past seventeen years. It has been my passion and hobby.

Working the night shift can be quite taxing on any individual, both physically and mentally. It is also the perfect shift for gauging how a new diet is working. Over the past ten years, I have tested various diets, habits, sleep schedules, all in the hope of finding the perfect combination to stay energized and healthy during a difficult shift. I have tried sleeping in three-hour blocks, being a strict vegan, being a strict vegetarian, trying a multitude of supplement combinations, fasting, snacking, and light therapy. I have come to one conclusion... There is no substitute for sleep.

Five years ago, I felt that I had hit on some breakthrough in my experiments for finding the perfect combination of these things to feel fully charged, all the time. I was literally jumping out of bed to start the day. I remember feeling so good and having so much energy, I felt like I was going to fly out of my shoes. Doing my best to maintain that feeling with my current diet and supplements at the time, it started to slowly degrade back to normal. Where I had been fine with sleeping only three hours in the morning and three hours at night to feel fully rested, I now required more solid sleep. There was no substitute for quality sleep. I'm sorry to report that I could not hack that.

Currently, I try my best to keep to that old regimen of a balanced diet of whole foods and proper sleep, supplementing where needed. But when you have a full household and need to make tasty, sustainable meals for more than just yourself, it can get tricky (expensive and time-consuming). Some people think I'm crazy when I mention that I fast for close to sixteen hours every day. I have one large breakfast when I get home from work around 9:00 am. Then a large dinner at around 5:00 pm and no food again until breakfast the next day. No snacks, only water and black coffee. If I get held over at work, I eat something quick. It helps to have a bag of emergency snacks with me in case I do go past 9:00 am, that way I don't kill anyone out of hanger. (No, that's not a typo).

As I've mentioned before, mental health issues are on the rise and they continue to cost us as a society. Apart from damages, injuries, and the cost of combating homelessness, drug addiction, and domestic abuse, mental illness also puts a strain on family members and friends who are trying to help those individuals in need. If you know someone, or you yourself are struggling with mental or emotional well-being, there are numerous resources for help. Two national hotlines - *Diamond Behavioral Help (844-755-5325)*, and *The 988 Suicide and Crisis Lifeline - Call or Text 988*.

5

A Different Way of Life

Prior to working as a police officer, my main job had been at our city's rescue mission. I started working in the homeless shelter, one department within a multi-building facility. It was an all-male shelter, and it was there that I learned more about mental illness than anywhere else. One usually assumes that when people find themselves homeless, it is for a short time. That they work and save up for an apartment, or one is provided for them and then they are no longer homeless and won't be homeless ever again. What I quickly learned was that homelessness is a condition of the mind and not of stature, for the most part. Men would come into our shelter for a few weeks to a few months, jump through hoops with the county and get their paid-for apartment. A few weeks, months, or a year later, they would trip up into old habits and find their way back to the shelter. It was a never-ending cycle. This is speaking on the individual who continues in negative behavior; those who do succeed and make the change are the complete reason I believe in the rescue mission and similar organizations. We do it for the success stories.

After my first day working in the shelter, I promised myself I would never find myself in that situation where I had nowhere to go. The shelter was cleaner than I imagined it would be, and that's due to the pride the residents and staff take in keeping it clean and tidy. But I wouldn't be able to fall asleep in a room full of people. I'm still not sure how these men did it for so long. The large room of bunk beds stays pretty noisy all night. But for most of these men, the shelter is cleaner and smells better than the conditions they had left, the conditions they let their apartment or room get to. It wasn't until I left the rescue mission and started working as a cop that I got to see how these people lived after they left the rescue mission. There are thousands of people in our country who just sleep on garbage on the floor. And when I say thousands, I don't mean like a low few thousand; I would say closer to a million. Numerous houses I entered while working on patrol were in a condition I couldn't live in for a day. And this was normal for them... sleeping on garbage, infested with bugs, with bites and rashes on their skin.

One morning, not too long ago, I arrived on the scene of an unattended death, meaning the person was found dead with no caregivers around and not in a hospital situation. He was just lying in a room of garbage. Moving large bags of cans and other refuse, I made my way to his body to check and verify if he was breathing. He was deceased and had rashes and bites all over his arms, chest, and neck. It looked like a skin-eating virus. I informed the sergeant on the street and started my part of the job of documentation and photographs. I asked his roommate for his name and almost fell over backwards when he told me. *Joseph Tremblay?* It couldn't be him. We rode the bus together for years in school. I was close friends with his brother. I used to party with Joseph when we were in high school. And it didn't look like him at all. I checked the date of birth, still not believing it was him. It was. I didn't know things had gotten so bad for him; how does one get to this point in his life? If he knew this was how it would end, would he change his ways? Do these people care if their bed was garbage? Upon closer look, I found wrappers of some synthetic drugs. Joseph's roommate said he had to get extremely high to get any sleep. I would, too, if I had to sleep in that room.

It appeared that Joseph had passed due to some medical issue, probably to do with the room he was sleeping in or the drugs he was taking. As I took my final photographs of his face, as difficult as that was, I went to move a black plastic bag that was near his mouth. The bag was stuck on his face. I began to pull and realized that it was stuck in his mouth. Jammed in his throat. Now every investigator who was on duty was going to be here; this was no longer a simple death scene. To this day, I don't know the outcome of the investigation. And I see his brother once a week at karate and still don't have an answer for him.

When I started at the homeless shelter, I hoped to eventually work my way up to the six-month rehabilitation program. I wanted to help people more long-term. In 2009, when I took the job, the men's shelter was at a low number... only about fifteen people. That holiday season, the population got down to eight. It was the lowest number of homeless men the shelter ever had; the numbers are now in the fifties and sixties. I completed my orientation and paperwork, and my new boss handed me my name badge on a blue lanyard. I quickly hung it around my neck and we headed into our staff meeting for the shelter and program staff.

The meeting consisted of about ten of us. We all sat in a circle on chairs and couches in the activity room of the rehab program, almost everyone had a hot coffee in a small Styrofoam cup. My new supervisor, Erick, started the meeting with an introduction of the newest hire. "We have a few items to get to in just a minute, but I wanted to introduce everyone to our newest member, who will be starting in the shelter, everyone welcome... Brian" *Oh*, I thought to myself, *they hired another person with me*. I looked around the room to find Brian, but all I saw were guys waving to me and saying 'hi.' I looked down at my name badge on my chest... Brian. *I guess I'm Brian now*. I started to think back on all the hiring paperwork I filled out. *Did I mess something up? Will this affect my taxes?* Erick continued on with his meeting while I planned how I would change my name to Brian... much easier than correcting everyone.

After the meeting, I got pulled into the office by our other supervisor, Daniel. "Erick, his name is not Brian!" Daniel exclaimed. "It's Alan." Erick looked at me and then looked down at my name badge. "Are you kidding me?" Erick said with a smirk, as if we were pulling some prank. I confessed to not correcting him and assured him my name was, in fact, not Brian. We all had a good laugh as I handed my name badge back. It was the first of many great laughs with those two and I would never work another job where I would laugh so much.

The rescue mission is a Christian organization that assists individuals struggling with homelessness and addiction. I thought I knew a lot about Christianity and homelessness, but I soon realized that I, in fact, knew very little. The people I would meet and the stories I heard over the next seven years were ones I would never forget. I was never quite in any danger like I am as a police officer, but there were many times I was put in a situation where I wasn't sure how to get myself out.

The shelter's overnight shift was my first time working through the night. At first, staying awake was the biggest struggle. I used to dread those days when the sun started going down, and I knew I couldn't sleep until the sun came up again. But then I started to love it. It was my time of peace. I sat in the dark in the tiny office connected to the large shelter room, the watcher of the homeless men awaiting the light of day. I steadied into a routine with the scheduled radio programs on a talk radio station and used my downtime, when I wasn't doing rounds, to read. I researched anything and everything, and experimented with writing funny stories based on the characters who came through our doors.

Occasionally, a resident who couldn't sleep would come in and want to talk. Most of the time, it was a short conversation. But some nights, we stayed up having in-depth conversations about the more intriguing things in life. Ghost stories, speculations about the spirit of man, bizarre things seen or talked about in other countries, conspiracy theory-typed talk. And just when I was getting comfortable with the darkness of night, the sun would be coming up and the other residents would be stirring. A quick breakfast with the guys in the dining hall and I was back home to sleep for the day.

It was in this position that I met one of the funniest guys I had ever known. Originally, I had taken him to be the most miserable person I had ever met. Short and stocky with a bald head and rough facial hair, Clayton had large circular rimmed glasses and took his time walking from place to place. "Give me my meds!" he demanded in his gruff voice when he first stepped into my office. His tone threw me off because no one had been that rude to me in a while. Clayton had a scowl on his face with his teeth half showing and one of his eyes squinted. I figured he was trying to act like a pirate. Clayton had eventually revealed to me that he was doing his best impressions of some of the shelter residents, although with a slight exaggeration. Clayton and I would have some of the best conversations at night when I was working, and I came to really admire the man for the way he saw the world.

Clayton stood apart from a lot of the shelter residents. One reason was that he worked full-time at a local McDonald's. He arrived back at the shelter late after work, sat and talked with me for a while, acted like he was miserable, and then went to bed. One night, I heard a series of loud rhythmic thumps outside of my office that sounded like they were coming from the other side of the wall. I stepped out to investigate and found Clayton sitting in the hall chair, banging his head hard against the office wall. "Clayton! What are you doing?" I asked.

"Oh, just trying to kill myself," he replied, so naturally as if he was telling me about taking a walk.

Clayton would occasionally mumble in his sleep; I'd hear him when I was doing my rounds. Sometimes it sounded like whimpering. I would hear him apologizing in his sleep and saying he missed someone. He would mention a female's name. When I asked him about it, he wouldn't speak to me, which always left me wondering if his act was just that or if maybe he was really hurting inside. I still look for Clayton at that McDonald's when I pass by, even though that McDonald's shut down years ago and is boarded up.

The rescue mission job was how I met one of my best friends, Luis. I didn't like Luis at first. He came into the homeless shelter office on shift change and sprayed everything with disinfectant and wiped down the keyboard and phones like I was a diseased, filthy animal. I think my first words to him were "I'm not sick", to which he replied "I always clean like this". Luis was a Spanish man, years older than me and about a foot shorter. But what he lacked in height, he made up for in his displays of authority and orderliness. He liked things clean and in a certain way and he wasn't slow to correct other staff members when he needed to. Luis was fluent in three languages – English, Spanish, and Microsoft Excel. He knew finances and spreadsheets better than anyone I ever met. The man grew up in New

York City in a wealthy household. He was very close to his mother and his brother. From accounts of what he told me, his mother ran the house. And even after she passed, the family was afraid to do anything that would upset her, as if she would come back from the dead to discipline them. Luis began to make money easily by doing things the wrong way in the city. He told stories about how he and his partner scammed some people, and about being shot at and threatened. Luis always loved telling the story about a guy who came into his office with a gun. From what Luis told me, he took the gun from the man after telling him he knew the man wasn't capable of shooting anyone, gave the man some of his bullets of the same caliber and said; *If you're going to shoot me, you use my bullets*. A week later, the man did shoot Luis... in the ass. "I have the scars to prove it," Luis would say as he pretended to pull down the back of his pants and laugh.

I liked Luis and came to think of him as an older brother. He guided me along and helped me with not only work issues but with things that were going on in my own life as well. I was still new and learning. Luis gave up the life of crime and moved to our smaller city. He wished for a simpler life and did not want to make more money than he needed to live on. No car, no house. He ran a long-term rooming house for only those who had graduated from the rehab program. And what a clean house it was! Luis would ask me for rides from time to time; for the most part, he didn't ask for much at all. He was about giving, even if it was the jacket he was wearing. Boy, did he have a way with the residents. They knew he meant business if he started to raise his voice. Ex-cons and the frequent homeless knew Luis and never wanted to be on his bad side. One morning, I saw him stand right up to a guy three times his size and threatened to sanction him from the county if he didn't get his act straight. It was like watching a cat get into a big dog's face and then seeing the dog walk away with its tail between its legs.

Luis made me laugh more than anyone in the world. We had one resident who came to us with an attitude issue. The man had one fake metal leg that he removed at night to sleep. One time, he decided he wasn't going to do his scheduled cleaning chores and just left his area a mess. That's a sure way to get on Luis's bad side! Luis took the man's prosthetic leg while he was sleeping and hid it. The guy had to hop to Luis's office and plead for his leg back. He never skipped his cleaning chores again.

We used to get lots of donations from the community that would sometimes come straight to our office. One new resident was nosy and always looking for things to take for himself. A nice, friendly couple donated a large box of cooking supplies one day, for residents leaving the shelter for a new apartment. The new resident came in and nosed around the box while Luis and I were talking. He picks up a metal pot.

"What's this?" he asks, as if he doesn't know.

"It's your pot to piss in," Luis said.

I almost hit the floor. I was laughing so hard. "Now you can't say you don't have one," I managed to get out.

A few years down the road, I transitioned to a full-time position in the rehab program, which was in the same building as the shelter. Luis and I were both on weekdays then. Fridays were our relaxation days, although every day felt like a relaxed day, really. We laughed all day long, it seemed, and I almost felt guilty taking a paycheck from the place. Our boss got upset and called me to his office one day. "Alan, Luis has been over to your office seven times today," he said. He was obviously keeping track... I'll bet he had less work than I. After that, we made it seem like we were working when we chatted it up. Luis yelled as loud as he could at me on the way out of my office, after we were done making jokes, to make it seem like he was cracking the whip on me about the finances. It worked. I also utilized the George Costanza method when Erick asked me how the finances were coming along. I rubbed my forehead and blew out a large breath, "It's coming."

One random day, Luis and I were conversing in my office, and he threw this out.

"Oh, I think I'm getting married next Friday."

"Well, what time? I think I'm moving to Japan that day," I joked, but I wondered what Luis was talking about.

"No," he laughed. "I'm serious. I asked Jeanette to marry me. We think next Friday is a good day."

"You're serious?" I replied. "Where and when?"

"It would be right after work in the chapel," Luis said. "Will you come?"

"Of course, I'm coming!" I told him. "Let me know what to bring and wear. That's great, man, congratulations." That was typical Luis. He never made a big deal about anything, and he never wanted to interrupt anyone else's plans or schedule. But, of course, I would clear my day even if I had plans. When the big day came, Luis was almost late for his own wedding because he worked almost up to the time of the ceremony and then got held up dealing with a disorderly resident. A short time later, Luis and his bride were married. It was a nice, small ceremony.

Luis tragically passed away during the Covid pandemic, and I found out too late. I never got to say goodbye to him, and it still hurts. He shows up in my dreams from time to time and he acts how he's always acted, like everything is going to be alright.

I still keep my ties with the rescue mission because I believe in what they are doing. I still hear from past residents who had gone through the doors - some multiple times - and then got it right and turned their lives around. They have restored families, new families, new careers, degrees, houses, two own their own business. To this day, about once every 6-8 weeks, I speak at the chapel of the mission and give parts of my story to share a message of encouragement. This keeps me grounded and humble. And although I hate to see that someone I knew fifteen years ago is still dealing with the same struggles, it's good to see a familiar face, and to see they are somewhere safe. The one change I have noticed over the years, however, is that the faces are getting younger.

After seven years at the rescue mission, it was time for me to go. Not that I wanted to. That was the best job and I would have loved to keep it for the rest of my life. But I was called to do more challenging things. The police exam was announced, and although I had glanced at it, I woke up from a dead sleep because something just told me that now was the time to take that test.

My last month at the rescue mission was one of the strangest. It coincided with a time when the city experienced a huge heroin and opioid issue. We had numerous residents in the shelter and rehab program undergoing medication-assisted treatment, or MAT, using a drug called suboxone, which, in my opinion, is just a legal, safer way for people to get high. Suboxone is a prescription medication for people withdrawing from heroin, and if you've ever witnessed someone going through withdrawals, you know that they need their medications like clockwork. Our medication dispersal system had been the same for years. There were two medication times for the residents, one in the morning and one at night. All medications were kept locked in a secure metal cabinet, which was locked in a separate room. The only people who had access to both keys were staff, and we were advised to always keep our keys with us while at work. Medications were checked for a proper count, usually every night, by the staff. We counted all the pills carefully and then put them back in their respective bottles. There were never any major issues besides a pill or two coming up missing. Some residents were quick with their hands, and when pills went missing, it was usually because they had taken extra doses of their own medication to get high.

Early one weekday morning, a staff member discovered that some suboxone was missing. I inquired how much. Seventy tabs/doses! This was an unheard-of amount! I was sure that there was a miscount or transcribing error. I checked the medication book myself and did a count. Sure enough, there were seventy tabs missing from the listed medication. I checked the number of the script and the medication box again – multiple times – still not believing it. Maybe there was a mess up with the pharmacy, I thought. But, no, that wouldn't account for our proper count when receiving the meds. We log them all in properly when they are delivered, before the resident even has access to them.

Everything was at a standstill until we let the boss know of our situation. Telling the resident his medication was missing right now was out of the question as well because we didn't know how he would act, or if he was even the suspect.

This was a big issue. I panned through hours and hours of security camera footage, watching residents and staff enter and exit the medication room together. We couldn't have cameras in the medication room. I came up with nothing. We switched to a new medication protocol immediately – only staff members were allowed in the room. All medications would be handed out from a tray to the residents in a hallway outside of the med room. We just had to remain vigilant to get the right meds on the tray. This took a lot of extra time and energy, but at least we knew no more medications would be pilfered by residents while they were in the room. We also possibly had staff to blame, as it came down to one or two who weren't paying attention enough to witness someone stealing out of the med cabinet.

A few days later, things had cooled down. I was sitting in Erick's office with another trusted staff member, and we were going over items to be worked on for the week. "So, no further issues with medications?" Erick looked at me.

"Are you asking me or telling me?" I looked up from my notes.

"Asking. Why don't you just go and double-check the count for the meds while we have some free time?" he motioned for me.

It was the last thing I wanted to spend my time doing after going through camera footage for the past few days, but I went to count the meds. Counting medications was one of my duties before I took over other responsibilities of the program, but it wasn't hard to jump back into it. It was a waste of time to count the lighter medications, like the vitamins or nerve suppressants. I went right for the suboxone, beginning with the resident's prescription who had come up missing. I started the count.

Off by eighty-four.

I counted again. Off by eighty-four. There must have been some mistake; we had rectified this issue. I checked the new scripts and the logbook multiple times. There was now another eighty-four missing, and that meant only one thing. Staff must be taking them. I suddenly got chills and wanted to get out of the medication room because now I was a suspect as well.

I walked into Erick's office with wide eyes and plumped down into the chair, not bothering to touch my coffee that

I had left on his desk. "Everything's still good, right?" Erick asked hopefully.

"No, no, everything is very far from good."

"What?" Erick looked like he was about to fall over. I didn't know what to say next and almost started laughing because it seemed so ludicrous.

"We are now missing eighty four suboxone," I told him. Erick gasped.

"How in the world..." he began.

This was now a campus-wide issue. Both Human Resources and the police got involved. We possibly had a staff member who was stealing pills or leaving his keys out for anyone to use. No damage was done to any locks, so unless a resident was able to pick locks or snag the keys while they were in staff possession...

Keys were confiscated and staff were not allowed in the med room until further notice. HR got "trusted" staff from another department to hand out our residents' medications. Meanwhile, I was preparing to jump ship as I had just gotten hired with the local police department, which probably did not look good in retrospect. Everyone knew me, though, and knew I was a health nut. I would have been the last person they would suspect of taking Suboxone. In reality, I wouldn't even know what to do with it. Most of the staff we hire were former residents who had at one point graduated from the program and showed a desire to come back to where it all turned around for them. I had always said they do a better job than I because they understand addiction. Seven years working in a shelter and rehab program and ten years as a police officer, and I still don't understand addiction. I'm not sure if they ever found out who had taken the medication, but that resident that had his come up missing left the program unannounced days later.

My last day of work came, and my coworkers and boss surprised me with a small going-away party with cake and everything. I tried not to tear up. The whole time, I was still worrying if I was making a huge mistake leaving the job I loved with the steady workweek and great coworkers. The cake was still on the table in the main activity room for anyone who wanted any. Early that morning, the police showed up – a newer officer and a seasoned investigator with the department. They were here to collect all of the video footage they could from our systems. I showed them the cabinet where all of our camera footage was stored and let them know I would be in my office if they had any questions.

A few minutes had gone by and the investigator came in to double-check the dates and times that I had recorded for our incident reports. "What's the cake for? Someone's birthday?" he asked.

"Oh no," I laughed. "The cake's for me; it's my last day."

"Awesome," he said. "What are you doing after this?"

"I'm coming to work with you."

6

The Start

Police academy day one, hour one. All the men and three women, dressed prim and proper, stood straight. Everyone seemed squared away, uniforms pressed and backs straight. Waiting in the hallway, I was both excited and nervous. I had no friends who had been through an academy, and I had no idea what to expect. It seemed I was the most underprepared mentally for what was to come. This day was a long time coming. It started three years earlier when I had first taken the civil service exam. That was before I developed this god- awful, pinched nerve in my leg. I couldn't stand or sit for more than an hour without immense pain, and I had no idea how I was going to sit through hours of academic classes or stand in a line to march, or whatever it was they were going to have us do. The battle to get here, however, had been so long and arduous that I was determined to see it through till the end, no matter what. If I passed out from the pain or died trying, I was going to muscle through every day. There was no giving up anymore.

I woke from a dead sleep early one summer morning with a heavy burden. The ad campaign had been background noise for the past few weeks. I had seen the "Join the Force" ad for the local Police Department, but paid it little attention. It must have filtered into my subconscious because I woke up that morning determined to apply for the test. I had made the promise to myself and to Jonathan's family that I would become a police officer. I knew I had put it off for too long. I dressed, made a quick breakfast, and drove down to city hall to pick up a test application. I carefully filled it out at home and returned it the next day. The test was two months away. Although I was a horrible test taker in school, I wanted to ace this exam, so I got ahold of a police exam practice book and jumped in. I spent three hours once a week in the local McDonald's taking a practice exam. I figured if I could get through a practice exam and do well with the constant distractions of the busy fast-food restaurant, I'd do even better in a quiet room for the real test. The day of the written test came, and I felt a rush of imposter syndrome. I was in a room with people who seemed a lot more qualified than myself. I was one of the first ones done with the test, but I left feeling defeated. The questions seemed so different from all my practice tests.

I waited a few long, agonizing months before I got the results back. I did phenomenal. Against all odds, I aced the test. A year later, there was a second test. I did well on that one, too, but I got a slightly lower score. Next was the physical test and I was hell-bent on acing that one, too. I was in relatively good shape, but I wanted to be a machine. The physical test consisted of pushups, sit-ups, and a one-and-a-half-mile run. At this time in my life, I had the full-time job at the rescue mission and was also working nights at a local Subway. Several days a week, I would leave my office at the mission and head to the college track. There, I would change into shorts and running shoes, do my run, pushups, and sit-ups in about half an hour, and then drive home to shower, change, and go to Subway to work the closing shift. I was burning the candle at both ends, but it paid off.

On the day of the physical test, I found myself in a gymnasium with a few hundred other people. Some of them appeared to be way more physically fit than me. I assumed everyone would pass the physical test. After all, everyone there had months to train and knew exactly what the physical test consisted of. I was wrong.

It seemed to me that most of these people hadn't trained at all. The pushups were not the hardest part; people failed the sit-up portion because they couldn't do them in time. When it came time for the run, I was pretty confident. These were my waters. There's not much I can say about the run... it was a run. So many people hated running, but I was having fun. By the time the test was over, half of the applicants had been eliminated. Those of us who were still standing received large packets – background packets – once we qualified. I had to write down – from memory – anything I had ever done. Once that was handed in, everyone's information was sent for background investigations, then interviews were set up. All of this was uncharted waters for me.

In all, I had about six interviews. In response to one of the questions I was asked, I told them I had recently seen a news article about Officer Johnson and how he was a true servant of the community, and that's the kind of officer I wanted to be. I didn't know Officer Johnson at the time, but a few years later, we would be great friends. After a three-year-long process, I finally made it to the last interview. The mayor called another candidate and me in and told us they only had one spot on the police department left to fill. He asked us who they should pick. I immediately knew that we were both getting hired, but apparently, the mayor thought we believed his joke, so he kept it going. I decided to look like the humble, generous guy, so I told the mayor to hire the other candidate. I took a bit of a risk, and my gamble paid off. We were both hired and would start in two weeks. I left City Hall that day and drove back to my office at the rescue mission on cloud nine. I had finally done it. Glenn Frey's song came on the radio, you know the one – "You belong to the city, you belong to the night." I had no idea then how true those words would be. I belonged to the city, and I would soon belong to the night shift. During my final days at the rescue mission, my pinched nerve got worse. I feared it would end my career before it began.

The weekend before I was to be sworn in, I had a trip to Florida planned with my best friend, Jack. The plane ride was terrible. I couldn't sit for more than an hour without the pain shooting up my lower back. I truly didn't think I was going to make it through the flight without asking if I could lie in the aisle for a while to ease the pain. I was sweating as we landed and was physically shot for that first night due to the pain. How I was going to make it through the academy, I had no idea.

On the first day of the academy, my only fear was that the pain in my leg and lower back would cause me to fail. A woman dressed in a uniform steps out into the hall with no emotion on her face. She said in a low, stern voice, "You have one minute to find your seats." It was silent for a moment while everyone waited to see if there were any further instructions. Then it was a mad dash into the classroom. Because no one knew anyone, we couldn't help each other. With seconds to spare, everyone found their seat. The two main instructors seemed miserable on the first day. It was so unlike any school class I'd ever been to. But they must put on that front. There are no games to be played in that classroom, and discipline is paramount. Despite the stern first impression, those instructors became the two people we looked up to during our time there. They put in the time to teach, correct, and care. I learned later on that this was one of the best academies in the state, and I could see why.

The morning session went smoothly, aside from the pain shooting up my leg. Luckily, the seats were padded, and we were afforded numerous breaks. I figured I'd actually be able to make it through this if every day were the same. We broke for lunch and were told when to return. Luckily, I didn't live too far away, so I shot home quickly for a bite to eat and some water, then headed back to the class.

The mood was eerie as I walked in. There was something not adding up about the way the instructors were just standing near the doorway. The newer instructors – at least, I took them to be newer – were standing near the edge of the room just staring us down. All seven of them. This is weird, I thought. As I got comfortable in my seat and listened to the speaker up front, another man was furiously pacing the room from right to left. I had no idea what the hell was going on, but I thought this was the most unusual class I had ever been in. This man was pacing and looking at everyone in the class like he wanted to kill us. What *the hell did we do?* I thought. The main speaker started to repeat himself, "Everyone just relax, we are just having a little talk. So, relax". *We are relaxed*. Well, I could at least speak for myself. I had no idea what this guy was getting at; things were going fine. But they weren't. Apparently, everyone else in the class had been warned about the first day, except me. We were about to do three hours of military drill outside.

The speaker, whom I came to know as one of the county's deputies and a long-time Police Academy drill instructor, suddenly switched gears. "We are going to go outside in a minute and do some drills," he said in a calm voice, almost a whisper. The man pacing around the room stood behind me. I felt him stop and breathe down my neck. "You have five minutes to be outside and lined up... GO!" the guy screamed. Then all of the other instructors off to the side started screaming as well. I thought I was in boot camp for a minute. Everyone was out of their seats and pushing through to the front door. I tried my best not to bump into anyone as we bottlenecked at the door. When I finally got out into the hallway, I could see other people, dressed in civilian clothes, lined up in the hallway. Some of them yelled at us, too. These people actually took time out of their day to watch this, like a show.

We got outside and lined up as they wanted us. We were wrong. The next three hours were filled with yelling, correcting, and name-calling. The instructors were all bigger than me and I knew it was only a matter of time before they were in my face. I had three of them on me at one time. I wasn't sure who to answer to. "Did I tell you to look at me?" one of them yelled. "Look straight ahead and answer him." I was getting conflicting orders. Part of me wondered how these guys could keep up with the yelling this long. I'd get tired. And to be clear, I'm not criticizing this part of the academy. I know now that it's crucial and I think it's a rite of passage. If you can't handle people yelling in your face, you won't last in the job. Looking back on it, I rather enjoyed it.

We were down on our faces and on our backs numerous times when we messed up, or just when the instructors felt like it. The pushups and sit-ups were no problem; I was good with any physical activity. It was only when I stood or sat for long that I was in pain. But then the instructor who had been pacing back and forth took over. I came to know him well as Sergeant Whitney with my department. I look up to him now and consider him a friend. The man would go out of his way to help anyone out. He started us on our backs with our legs straight out and lifted a few inches off the ground. I felt like I could hold this position forever. Sergeant Whitney was holding the position with us as well, and also laughing at the recruits who were already struggling. "I'm over forty and doing these exercises and you kids can't even keep your legs up?" he shouted. A minute must have passed by. I started to feel the burn in my upper leg and butt. That sharp pain was starting to come through as well. A few seconds later, I could feel that pinched nerve all the way from my foot to my lower back.

I tried to hang on as long as I could. But I finally threw in the towel. *If I couldn't keep my legs up on day one*, I thought, *if this pinched nerve causes this much pain every day, I'm not going to make it to the end.* My leg was burning as I fought myself. I heard my colleagues breathing heavily. They were fighting the burn as well, but theirs isn't the same pain I felt.

Just when I thought I couldn't stand any longer, I felt a pop where my femur meets my hip, as if a bone shifted slightly. And immediately... relief! My legs were still burning from the workout, but the sharp nerve pain was gone. "Okay, drop 'em," Sergeant Whitney called out. Everyone sighed. "Back on your feet!" No rest.

I stood, moving my right foot slightly to see if the pain was truly gone. That dull ache that had been there for months had left. I forgot what normal felt like. Another drill instructor was now in my face. He knew I wasn't paying attention to what they had ordered us to do. But I didn't care. I felt normal again. As the instructor yelled, I tried not to smile.

After a few more drills, it was time to call it a day. The first academy class came to an end, and we were dismissed until tomorrow. I had to cut my hair and shine my boots better; I also had a headache from being in the sun all afternoon. Part of me was skeptical that the pain would come back once I lay down for the night.

The next day started bright and early with military drill. We had Sergeant Whitney again as our main instructor that day. And we were back to doing pushups and leg lifts. I was grateful the nerve pain hadn't returned. Then I was caught not calling out with my four-count pushups properly, and Sergeant Whitney had me sit on the wall until he said I could come back. Sitting on the wall entailed putting my back up against the exterior wall of the building with my knees at a ninety-degree angle, as if I were sitting in an imaginary chair. If you've ever done this exercise, you know it's great for your core, abs, and upper legs. But it is a killer. However, there I sat, fighting the burn but entirely happy that my pinched nerve was taken care of. And I had Sergeant Whitney to thank for it. Maybe one day, I'll tell him he saved my career.

As severe as the pain had been, I never saw a doctor for it. I can only guess it was a sciatic nerve that somehow got pinched, possibly from the way I had been sitting for several years in an office chair. The important thing is that the pain never returned.

The rest of the academy went great. I started to enjoy military drill, especially when other people were getting yelled at. The things these instructors would say... it became more of an endurance trial not to laugh. Three recruits quit that first week and they hired a new guy who was, fortunately, more uncoordinated than me. A few times, I had to hold the laughter in by clenching my fists or biting my lip. If we didn't have military drill, we had the hardest cardio I've ever had in my life. I was used to cross-country practices when we would run close to ten miles every day, so the running part was a piece of cake. Most days, I was breathing through my nose after four or five miles. But the cardio in the gym and on the grass was brutal. I started to lose muscle mass from all of the calories I was burning. I tried supplementing my breakfasts with ice cream every day to keep the calories up, but that was foolish. Pushups started to become difficult because of all the mass I was losing. Where I could once easily do sixty, I was now struggling at thirty.

Emergency vehicle operations training was fun. I already considered myself a great driver at high speeds from years of playing Grand Theft Auto, and I could easily park a large vehicle with my steamroller experience. I've always been comfortable behind the wheel. Firearms were only a struggle due to the July heat and being stuck in gear (mostly black) all day. This was coincidentally the last time I had a cold that lasted for more than a few days. The training was held for a full two weeks. It was rough... every day out in the sun, struggling to breathe properly. A few times, I thought I was going to pass out on the firing line. Once everything was said and done, I seemed to have sweated out all of the toxins in my system. It was probably the healthiest I had ever been in my life. I promised myself I would bulk up and get my muscles back after the academy. Now it was time for the real work.

It's always the same statement I hear people make – "I don't know how you do it." Once I got through the academy, the job itself seemed easy. Everything has its set order and procedural guidelines. Anyone can get used to the paperwork. Violent situations account for only a fraction of the job, and sorting the chaos into a sound structure is something that gets easier with time. The toughest part of the job is making sure you don't make a mistake and get your superiors upset with you or let down the person you're trying to help.

After ten years on the job, you'd think the most dangerous moments would be the ones that haunt me at night. Strangely, they're not. I've yet to have any bad dreams about the things I've experienced. Instead, I have nightmares about being a waiter again, struggling to catch up on my tables, or being in college again and I have a project due in a few hours but can't seem to figure out where to start. Is it crazy that I wake up from these dreams, I think, *oh, thank God, I'm not in school again! I just have to get up and go to a job where people want to hurt me?* Where are we as a society when social constraint is a heavier burden than personal safety and well-being?

I will admit I was a late bloomer. Starting my career in law enforcement at age 31 has had its advantages and disadvantages. In the first few years, people thought I had been on the department longer than I had been because I looked older. But now, officers who are my age are retiring and jumping into their next career. I had many jobs before this one, however. I wore a lot of hats – quite literally. The combined experience of all of those other jobs worked to my benefit when it came time to jump into police work.

I mowed lawns at a young age for a local church, shoveled snow, delivered newspapers, worked retail, fast food, coffee shops, on a farm, in two restaurants, and finally as a counselor and program supervisor at the rescue mission. Some occupations require more flexibility than others. No job I've ever had has required more flexibility than being a police officer. On any given shift, I might find myself acting as a counselor, chauffeur, dog wrangler – or cat wrangler – a couple's therapist, a bearer of bad news or good news, a plumber, a stand-in parent, a friend, a car-battery jumper, or even a secretary.

As far as dangers of the job, they are numerous. Officers put their lives on the line every day, all over the country. We deal with the mentally unstable – who may or may not have a weapon – we assist the fire department with fires, chemical spills, and gas leaks, we deal with rabid animals, aggressive canines, broken glass, traffic collisions, exposure to viruses, and the mental and physical strains of the job itself. Then most officers still have to go home and be a spouse, parent, coach, teacher, leader, provider, cook, and home caretaker.

I've been fortunate in my career so far to have only had a few minor injuries sustained on the job. In my very first year on the force, I responded to a domestic dispute in which a woman dumped all of her clothes on the stairway before she left the apartment. I didn't watch my footing and fell. My boot got caught in the strap of a bra, causing me to trip. I was falling headfirst down a long stairwell, but I threw my head back to turn my body around. Putting my arms out to stop my fall was a big mistake. I gripped the stairs below me to keep myself from falling all the way down the stairs, but my body continued to fall as my left arm stayed put. The result: a pulled tendon in my shoulder.

I never reported the injury. I was still new, and I didn't want to be seen as a liability to the department right off the bat. So, I kept it hidden. I drove with one arm for months. As soon as my shoulder started to heal, something would happen at work to strain it again – moving something heavy or wrestling with someone. It wasn't until I switched my diet around and dropped the sugar, dairy, and processed foods that it began to heal. In just two weeks, I went from not being able to do one pushup to moving my arm in any position without any pain. The injury never returned.

The next eight years, I was accident and injury-free. Just this past year, while in the process of detaining a man, I tore the UCL in my thumb. The subject jerked his arms back really fast, causing my thumb to bend backwards. It swelled up to the size of a golf ball within seconds of the injury. I possibly needed surgery to repair the ligament, the doctor explained. My department planned for me to be off work until the end of summer, but I made a surprisingly fast recovery. I was able to move my hand properly within three weeks. The doctor still didn't feel safe having me return to full duty, so I humbled myself and became a light-duty officer for a little over a month. I thought I was going to dread it, but I ended up enjoying it. For several weeks, I worked in the property room with the property officer – an officer who had been in this position since I joined the force. I just knew her as the evidence officer who sent emails when you labeled property wrong.

Rows and stacks and bags of property lined the evidence room. There must have been at least a million pieces of evidence in that one room alone... and there were three other storage rooms for evidence. Every day, I went through five bins of evidence – each containing anywhere from 20 to 250 pieces of evidence. If it was old and the case was completed, it could be thrown out. Everything had to follow a set process outlining how it was to be destroyed or discarded. There were thousands of people's old belongings – purses, cell phones, lighters, clothes, pocket knives, and a can of creamed corn in a sock (probably used in an assault). There were also thousands of spent bullet casings, projectiles, and fragments from hundreds of scenes. I could now see why managing evidence was a full-time job, and I gained respect for the property officer in any department who has that responsibility. The only person I managed to piss off during my time in the evidence room was the maintenance guy, who shook his head every time I came out with another full bag of trash for him to take to the dumpster.

My latest on-the-job injury occurred just a month ago. I responded to a domestic dispute between a mother and her adult son. He was about twenty-five years old, still living at home, and had issues with drugs and alcohol. When I first arrived on scene, the son, Carmine, was flippant and his emotions were high. After a few moments, I calmed him down and saw that his anger stemmed from an argument with his mother. He admitted that he pushed her and that he knew that was wrong. I told him that his frustration may not only be with his mother, but that he was still sharing a house with her, and that their relationship might get better if he moved out. We had a good rapport while talking with each other and he shook my hand numerous times.

At first, the mother wanted him arrested, but then she changed her mind. He had no prior criminal history and she hesitated to put a charge on him. I agreed with her that that might be best and started a report for her on the domestic dispute. When I came back into the house, however, Carmine had completely changed character. He was slurring his words and almost falling over. I then learned that he had taken a large quantity of pills prior to my arrival. My hands were now tied; he had to go to the hospital for ingesting the pills. Carmine refused to go anywhere. He started flailing his arms around. For safety reasons, he had to be detained until he could get to the hospital.

Handcuffing Carmine was no problem; what came after was the difficult part and a hard lesson to learn. Someone in handcuffs can still pose a safety risk to themselves and others. Carmine began to thrash around on the ground as I tried to hold his legs. I was worried he was going to smack his head against the wall. Carmine threw his head back and almost hit me, then he moved over to my left arm. I thought I could hold him from there, but I felt pressure on my left bicep. It surprised me at first; I didn't think someone would actually bite me. The pain increased by the second as he bit down harder – and would not let go. I screamed from the pain as I tried to hit his head away from my arm. The man had such a grip with his teeth that it only hurt me more than it hurt him. I finally pulled out my taser and was about to send a jolt to this guy when he released his bite, headbutted me, and thrashed on the floor again.

I was momentarily stunned, but went back to work, trying to hold him down. "You're treating me like an animal!" he yelled. "Because you're acting like an animal!" I yelled back. "You freaking bit me."

I held the taser to his stomach as he stared at me with eyes that were more intense than his bite. He kept taunting me to tase him. A few seconds later, Carmine suddenly sat up and lunged – with his mouth open – towards my neck, making chomping noises like a cartoon character getting ready to bite someone. It was horrifying. I was worried he was going to latch onto my face or bite my nose off. Carmine got what he wanted. The taser made a loud 'click, click, click, click' noise that made Carmine stiffen up and try to get away. Regret finally set in on him as he screamed for it to stop. I asked him if he wanted to get tased again. This time, he said no.

I was back to work three days later with my arm wrapped up. The bite still looks nasty and I will probably have a scar there for the rest of my life. More than likely, I will see Carmine again in the course of my career. And I hope it's a warm night when I'm wearing short sleeves and can show him where he bit me, to remind him of what drugs can do to someone. But more than that, I hope to see him when I'm not working, like in a social setting. And maybe we can have a laugh over it. Although I was extremely pissed in that moment of panic and pain, I let it go before I left that call. Ultimately, I know what he did wasn't personal. I don't hold anything against him for it. Forgiveness, I've come to find out, is the strongest weapon a police officer can use. It protects you when you leave work and head home. It keeps you from becoming the irate, grudging, bitter people that we sometimes have to deal with. And frankly, holding grudges as an adult is childish. But I learned my lesson that night. Anyone can be dangerous in any environment.

7

DOMESTICATED

It was just another quiet and seemingly normal night as I was doing my rounds through my zone. A couple, however, had been arguing for hours in their apartment at the edge of my patrol area. The argument escalated to a dangerous point when the pair moved the argument outside and the woman tried driving away. The man, attempting to stop his girlfriend from leaving, jumped onto the moving vehicle. Whether out of anger or fear, I do not know, the woman drove aggressively to get her boyfriend off of the vehicle, ultimately resulting in the man being thrown off and onto the pavement. I wasn't sure which of the two parties had called 911, but there was a report that a man was down on the ground and injured, and paramedics were en route.

When I got there with my partner, Watson, we found the man sitting down on the dirty pavement and clutching his foot with his hands. There was blood on his fingers and he was crying out in pain. We asked him what happened and he told us that when he fell off the vehicle, his foot struck the pavement hard and he thought he had broken a toe. The man removed his hands to reveal a middle toe that had been almost snapped off. My partner and I winced at the sight. It was the type of sight you expect to find after you stub your toe really hard and believe you'll have a toe missing. The poor man's toe was only hanging on by some skin, just dangling from his foot.

I told him he was going to have to go to the hospital and that's when he started to panic and protest. "I'm not going, I don't want to go, I'll just pull it off and be done with it." The man immediately sat back up and began reaching for his dangling toe. Watson and I looked at each other briefly in fright at the thought of this man pulling his toe off in front of us. We quickly grabbed his arms and held him back. We told him that it was a horrible idea and not to look at his toe and just let the hospital fix it.

Luckily, he came to his senses and agreed that going to the hospital was the better option. He knew that hanging onto a moving car had been a horrible idea and didn't fault his girlfriend for the incident. Watson looked at me as the ambulance pulled away. "I thought he was going to pull that thing off in front of us," he said.

"I know, I don't think I would have ever been able to forget that if he did." A shiver went down my spine thinking about it. I got back into my car and parked around the corner to start my report.

Domestic disputes are among the most common calls we handle, and they often follow a frustrating pattern. In many cases, the problem isn't just a single argument – It's an ongoing cycle. Both parties remain in the relationship even though it's clearly unhealthy. More often than not, they are more comfortable staying together and continuing to fight than facing the difficult step of living apart.

Most domestic disputes are ridiculous. Dealing with these incidents is how I realized that people can call the police for anything. "*My boyfriend won't stop tickling me and I just want to go to sleep.*" "*Okay, sir, do you mind not tickling her for the rest of the night?*" "*My girlfriend wants me out of the house so she can have someone else over.*" "*My wife covered me in mustard because I called her a pig.*" You do what you do the best you can to keep the peace. The hopes that people would step outside of their feelings and walk away are always high, and it is always a letdown. But that's how it is when just one person needs to have the last word, and that's when things get escalated.

One domestic was an older married couple that lived together with their seven cats. They split a large bottle of vodka most nights (the married couple, not the cats) and then would have outrageous arguments. When I showed up with my partner, Wilson, the two were each on their own side of the sectional couch, drunk and with their feet touching. "*She keeps kicking me and I want her to stop!*" Sometimes you have to remind yourself that you're not on a T.V. show, that you're dealing with grown-ups and not children. Growing up, I could never have imagined myself as a fifty-five-year old adult who decided to call the cops on my wife for kicking my feet while we were lying on the couch. And these people don't see anything wrong with that. A lot of the time, they end up siding with each other while we are still there and turn on us. It's ironic and comical, but can be dangerous.

One woman I deal with about once a month illustrates perpetual calling perfectly. Each time I respond to a call from her, she doesn't remember that I'm the same officer she has spoken with many times before. She tells me she wants her boyfriend out of the house and that she's afraid of him. She has been saying the same thing for the past four years. During that time, she has even moved twice – with him.

Over the years, I have carefully explained the steps she could take if she truly wanted to leave the relationship. I've provided phone numbers and information for emergency housing and support services. Each time, the information is acknowledged and then ignored.

I never want to make light of domestic violence – it is a serious and dangerous problem around the country, with victims from any age, gender, race. The unfortunate thing is that the people who do need the help to get out of these abusive relationships are reluctant to reach out. Most of law enforcement's time spent on "domestic violence" is spent with people who just don't know how to stop arguing, usually familiar couples who call frequently.

Although breaking up arguments can be an arduous process, there is one couple who never fails to put a smile on my face. The elderly man and his wife live on the edge of my zone. The man has a walker and moves very, very slowly. His wife has a habit of wandering the streets at night

– doing God knows what – before she comes home and starts an argument with her poor husband. She is usually the one to call the police and she always claims that her husband is trying to hurt her. One night, she told dispatch that her husband grabbed a pair of scissors and was chasing her around the apartment. Yes, the husband who needs help getting up from his couch and leans on a walker to keep from falling! She is always kind and gracious enough to open the door for me because she knows her husband has mobility issues and sits on his couch watching T.V. all night.

"She's back at it again?" I asked the man who is now familiar with me.

"I don't know what she smoked, but she came home and started throwing things around," he replies, not taking his eyes from his T.V. show.

"Did you chase her around the apartment with a pair of scissors?" I asked.

That's when the man looks at me sideways. "Do I look like I can chase anyone around my apartment?"

The man and I usually spend a few moments conversing and sharing a laugh about his wife's recurring outbursts before I leave for the night. As for the wife, she usually calms down rather quickly and becomes friendly and polite. She typically shows me to the door and thanks me for stopping by, as if I'm just a guest over to visit.

I was on my way to a reported physical domestic in the north part of town, the nice part. A woman had called 911, claiming her boyfriend had beaten and strangled her, and she was afraid of what he would do next. She mentioned wanting him out of the apartment. I arrived to find the girl standing outside with her arms folded and in tears. She told me a detailed story about how her boyfriend stays inside all day, plays video games and won't find a job. She came home from work and tried to talk to him about his motivation issue. The boyfriend got irate and pushed her, punched her a few times, and then put his hands around her neck and squeezed until she got away and called the police. At this point, I didn't need to hear anymore; I was ready to arrest the guy.

"I just want him out of the house," she said as I walked toward the front steps.

"You don't want him arrested, after all he did?" I asked.

"Whatever will make him stay away the longest," she answered, in a slight accent. I pegged it as either Russian or Polish. "My mom is on her way here now. If he won't go, I will just stay with her."

I knocked on the front door, and the man called out for me to come in. As I step inside, I see him sitting on a couch with a large flat screen television propped up on the coffee table. He has video games stacked up next to his feet. The whole time, I'm thinking *this guy must have some balls to just sit there, knowing I was called here for what he just did to his girlfriend.* The man barely took his eyes from the screen to look up at me. "You know why I'm here?" I ask sternly.

"Yes, sir," he replied. "She probably said I hit her or something. I have a recording of her saying she was going to call you guys and lie to you."

"Really?" I was intrigued.

He pulled out his cell phone and pressed play on a recording that was time-stamped from just about twenty minutes earlier. I heard the girl's voice as the two were arguing. "Well," she began. "I'll get you out of here. I'll just call the cops and tell them you hit me and choked me, and they will believe me cause I'll cry. And they will arrest you and you won't be back." Her tone of voice was so... Assured. It made me mad. She just cried to me and put on a performance, and I believed her. I was all set to arrest this guy and it would have been on this girl's pony show.

"Do you want to hear the rest of it?"

"No, sir," I replied. "I've heard enough. Sorry to bother you tonight." With that, I stepped outside.

There she was, standing next to her mother, crying. It made me sick. "Miss, can I talk to you over here?" I motioned. "I don't think your mom wants to hear what I have to say."

The girl walked with me toward my patrol car, and I started in on her. "You know what you did. If you ever pull that again, I will arrest you for making a false police report. My best advice to you is to go with your mother tonight and move out of the apartment if you don't think you can make things work with your boyfriend, but don't get us involved unless you really need us." She started in with excuses, but I just walked away and got in my car. Sadly, this wasn't the only time I've caught spouses or girlfriends lying about things to get their significant other locked up. Luckily, she never called again, at least not while I was working. She either moved out or the two reconciled their differences.

A trusted flashlight is a must for the night shift. Sometimes even the best flashlight can fail just when you need it the most. The piece of garbage I had with me now was faulty; it would shut off for no reason and usually at the worst times. We got a call just around 4:00 am. A woman stated that she was being held at gunpoint by her ex-boyfriend, who broke into the apartment. She claimed she was in the bathroom with the door locked and that he was in the apartment and wouldn't leave. Seven officers arrived on scene within a matter of minutes. I got up the stairs with our sergeant and two other officers. We climbed the staircase to the third floor and knocked. No answer. Knocking harder and more frequently usually gets someone to finally answer. When we did that this time, a female's voice answered. We told her who we were and that we needed to make sure everyone was alright. She yelled at us through the door that she was okay, but was not opening the door for police and that she wanted us to leave.

In these circumstances, we can't just walk away, even if someone's telling us they are okay. The boyfriend could be in there with a gun pointed at her, telling her he will shoot if she doesn't get the cops to leave. We have to actually see the person and make sure no one is inside with a gun. You may be wondering if our presence could make things worse for someone if we don't leave. Well, If her boyfriend was there with a gun and she wished for us to leave, who is to say that he won't shoot her anyway if we go? As most of these domestics go, they usually don't get better if we leave.

These are the unknowns, so the best practice is to make sure everyone is all set before departing. So, we continued arguing through the door.

The sergeant calmly called back, "Go to my car and get the shield." I had no one behind me blocking my path, so I ran down quickly and retrieved the ballistic shield. I didn't even think to ask if he wanted it for himself and figured I would just hold it at the front and be the first to enter. The shield can be a burden sometimes if you have to enter a tight space quickly.

I waited at the top of the stairs, holding the shield between myself and the door in case bullets came flying through. The sergeant continued to talk with the woman and tell her why we were there. She swore up and down that no one was inside with her, that she didn't call, that she had just gotten out of the shower. After close to twenty minutes, she finally unlocked the door and let us in. I went through first with the shield and my gun at the ready. The woman was in a towel and her two small children were standing in the main living room, looking up at us curiously but seemingly unafraid. This was unusual company for them at this hour. All we had to do now was make sure no one else was in the apartment and we could go.

We cleared all the rooms easily within a minute and ended up in a rear bedroom that was empty. I peered out of the windows to the ledges to see if anyone was waiting outside. I've found people hiding out on rooftops before when they knew we were coming. The only other thing that was in the room was a long cord hanging from the ceiling. It was to attic steps. One of the guys I was with pulled the cord down as he held our guns towards the opening. I figured the chances of someone being up there were minimal, but still, there could be no chances taken when dealing with someone with a gun. I wanted to be the first one up there to check it out because my adrenaline was up and, to be truthful, my favorite part of the job was going into unknown buildings and rooms looking for someone.

I tried, at first, to go up the steep, tiny steps with the shield, but found it to be more troublesome than it was worth. So, I handed the shield off and decided I was going to have to take the chance without it. Halfway up the steps, I got my flashlight out and started to shine it around, keeping my gun low. My head popped up from the attic opening first. I made sure to look behind me and to the sides first and clear that area. Then I got fully up into the attic and peered down to the end. The attic went the entire length of the building and had no flat floor to walk on, just boards of wood and insulation that felt like it would give way and drop me crashing into the apartment below.

I made my way with just my flashlight shining towards the far end. I saw what appeared to be a ball of laundry at the far end, lying between two of the boards. When I called out that I was the police and for anyone to announce themselves, I saw the laundry pile move slightly. I immediately realized it was a person's back. That was the moment my flashlight suddenly shut off. It was pitch black, and I couldn't see a thing. The person could be lunging for me or shooting at me and I wouldn't know unless I heard something. I panicked and smacked the flashlight as hard as I could on my palm. No luck. Then I shook it vigorously and it kicked back on, flickering. I pointed it back at the man who was now kneeling, facing me. "Show me your hands!" I yelled. He lifted his hands. I had him turn around and show that he had no weapons on him, then commanded him to slowly walk towards me.

The man almost fell through the floor on his way to me. I told him to be careful as he got closer. When he was a few feet away, I reached for him to help him to the steps. The handcuffs were not going on until we got him to the steady floor of the apartment. We couldn't risk someone falling and getting injured. Besides, as of this moment, he had committed no crime and was only suspected of having a gun. Once he was down, the other officers made sure he had no weapons hidden away anywhere after handcuffing him. I thoroughly searched the attic for a gun but couldn't find one.

Back on the main floor, we talked further with the couple. The man said he hid because of the way we were knocking and kicking the door. He thought he was going to jail for something, but didn't know what. We spoke with the woman for some time and found out that the two had argued with another woman friend a few hours ago. That other woman was apparently our caller posing as the man's girlfriend and making up the story about the gun. Some people do that... more than you'd think. They want to get someone else in trouble and they call in some fake information, hoping for the worst. All information has to be looked at, and from different angles before we know what's going on.

I purposely excluded most of the violent domestic calls for a reason. There is enough of the violent and tragic, especially at the beginning of this book. I didn't feel that there needed to be any more to get my point across. The truth of the matter is that people are injured and killed every day as a result of domestic violence, both male and female. Children are almost always affected; if they are not the victims, then they are left without one parent, or both. My jurisdiction deals very strongly with domestic violence and abuse. I can only speak for my area. We have numerous outlets, programs, and resources for victims, and domestic incidents are one of the most scrutinized when it comes time to review incidents. People who are mentally unstable/unwell and looking to hurt someone besides themselves will usually go to the person or people they are closest to.

If you are or know someone who is a victim of domestic violence, please don't hesitate to get in touch with the resources in your area. Or you can call the *National Domestic Hotline - 800-799-7233*. Sometimes all it takes is that first step.

8

The Grid

"I'm calling the cops!" The man shouted from his bed, half under the covers. He was a very young, short, Hispanic man we had been dealing with more frequently as of late. He had a history of getting drunk and then calling the police or having the police called on him. Just last week, I found him stumbling near the road outside of the diner I cooked at on the weekends. I moved him onto the sidewalk and called for an ambulance to take him to the hospital because he was drooling and bleeding from his nose from some unwitnessed injury. Then he took a swing at me. I put him in handcuffs and pinned him up against the glass door of the diner to keep him from falling or hurting himself. A short, drunk man can be very easy to keep under control if they aren't hyped up. It was like keeping a lethargic child from wandering into the road. The next day, I stopped at the diner for breakfast and only then noticed the blood on the glass door. After the paramedics took him to the hospital, I hadn't seen him until the night he shouted that he was calling the police from his bed. "We are the police," I responded to the man. I glanced at the other officers I was working with, trying not to laugh. We were standing in the man's room, and obviously we would not even be there if he hadn't called 911 – repeatedly – saying that he was in danger. He had refused to give our dispatchers his address or anything else; he was just in the business of making these bizarre calls once a week. It took us a while to find his apartment. A quick call to the property manager of the building and we were able to ascertain his apartment number. He hadn't locked his front door and we had every reason to enter his apartment as he said he was in "danger."

"I'll call the other police!" he yelled. "And they will come and arrest you for being in my room!" His whole body shook like one of those tiny dogs that puts its whole body into a bark.

"Are you in danger, sir?" I asked, already knowing the answer.

"No! Get out, get out, get out!"

"If you don't want police in your apartment, sir, don't call them and say you're in danger," I replied as we stepped out of the bedroom to leave. It seemed so simple to me. But this wasn't an isolated incident. This happens more often than most people realize. People call the police and yell at them for showing up, or threaten to call other police on them. All I could do was shake my head. It was back to my car to type my report and continue on with the night.

There is no rhyme or reason to the calls you can go to in a shift. Generally – and I use that term loosely – we are slower in the winter than in the summer. I have said, after a few winter months, that I could work this job every night for the rest of my life. Then summer comes around. The warmer nights bring their own unique and unexpected challenges. But nothing is predictable. I've had extremely busy night shifts on a random Tuesday in the winter and really slow Friday night shifts in the summer. You just never know what you're getting when you go into work.

Don't get me wrong; I don't regret the job one bit. I am grateful for every night I get to wear the uniform. The day I don't feel like I'm helping anyone is the day I will hang up my hat. But to drudge through a night of nonstop calls, then head home to focus on home life issues and balance a separate social life, can burn someone out fast if they are not careful. You need at least one full day of rest a week.

Many times, my family and friends know what's going on in the city before I do. I usually don't check social media or my text messages until after my shift. When I wake at 10:30 pm to get ready for work, I keep my phone in my pocket and miss the latest news. So it's not until I pull into the lot and see all the extra cars and walk into the station to see everyone busy in the work station, that I find out about a recent homicide.

After each call, it is back to the streets. My grid – the section of the city I worked for the past six years – is a .6 by 1.1 mile grid of mostly duplexes, single-family houses, and a few apartment buildings. The grid is almost a perfect rectangle, shaped like Colorado, near the center of the city. Despite its relatively small size, it is home to a lot of the people who frequently call the police for various reasons. Over the years, I've gotten to know the same faces and the same houses. I like this section of the city because the calls are usually not some nonsense –like 'my neighbor left his trash bin too close to my driveway' or 'I'm getting phone calls from numbers I don't know and I'm too lazy to block them.' Instead, in this area of town, we get calls from 'regulars.' There is one woman, for example, who calls the police almost every week when her boyfriend acts up. She never actually wants us to respond, and when we do, she refuses to talk to us. Once, she yelled at us for being in her house after her mother let us in. She uses the 'I'm going to call the police on you' trick to keep her boyfriend in line. It is a threat, like when a younger sibling says they are going to tell mom and dad – even though they never do.

Aside from the people, I like the grid because nearly all the streets are straight. It makes it easy to get from one call to the next. But I also like this area because there are a lot of unusual things that happen in my zone – most of the stories in this book came from my grid. On one recent wintery night, for instance, I started my shift driving down every street in a row – as I normally do in my first hour – and I saw a guy riding a bicycle along the side of the road. Not an unusual sight at all. What caught my attention, however, was when the man glanced back at my patrol car briefly... I was still a few yards behind him. The man looked frightened, turned back to his handlebars, and rode a few more feet. Then he hopped off his bike and into the snowbank.

From where I was sitting in my patrol car, it looked quite comical. I thought it was some kid messing around because the cops were behind him. I pulled up to the man in the snowbank, and with my window rolled down, I asked him what he was doing with the tone of a parent asking a toddler why they are making a mess. I got no answer. I noticed the man was barely moving. I still thought he was playing a game – playing possum – so I sat there for a moment waiting for him to jump and say, "got ya!" But something didn't feel right.

After a few more seconds, I got out of my car, went over to the guy and shook him. "Hey, buddy?" I asked. "You okay?" No response. I shook him a little harder and rolled him over. I noticed he had a minor cut on his forehead – probably from the fall into the snow and ice – and his eyes were still open. His breathing was shallow. I called for medical services on my radio and started CPR. Luckily, an ambulance wasn't far away and got there quickly. They took over the CPR and transported him to the hospital a few moments later. Before they did, my sergeant pulled up to see what was going on. He saw my vehicle parked in the road and a bike rider on the ground, not moving. His first thought was that I hit the guy with my patrol car. I panicked. *My goodness, it must look like that! I hope there are cameras in the area that caught this whole thing.*

At the hospital, the nurses and doctors did their best to perform life-saving measures, but the man's condition deteriorated fast. They were unsuccessful. The man died. The doctor said it appeared to have been a heart attack that caused the man to die so suddenly, but they wouldn't know for sure until after an autopsy. Part of me was worried that I had scared him to death just by being on the street. Wrong place, wrong time.

Every day, police officers deal with chaos that must somehow be sorted into a workable sense of order. We respond to people wronging others, people in places they shouldn't be, and people complaining about any number of things. Many of these situations stem from the same root causes: people are unable to control their emotions, their alcohol intake, or both.

I'm only going to speak for myself here... the job is mostly talking to people. Now, every department and every situation could be different. On average, I speak with between three and twenty-five people in a given night, depending on how busy it is. I already know the majority of these people from past calls or from the rescue mission, so that makes my job way easier. Sometimes all people want is someone to listen. I've been to plenty of calls in which the person was able to come to their own solution to their problem just by talking it out. Don't get me wrong; there are plenty of calls in which a person involved refuses to listen to anything that is said, and that's where things can get difficult. Usually, it is a call involving drugs, alcohol, and emotional instability. A lot of people don't realize that they can resolve an issue by just walking away. I've lost count of how many times I've responded to a scene where a caller simply wants someone – who doesn't live there – to leave. When that person refuses, it often ends in a trespassing arrest or escalates into a confrontation with police or others on scene, leading to additional charges. All because they didn't want to walk away.

Back on the grid, the sun was starting to peek up over the hill after a slow night. There weren't any calls in the two hours before dawn. The calls started coming in once people started waking up to find their teenager had snuck out of the house sometime in the night, their car door was open, a wallet was missing, and there was someone they didn't know sleeping on their front porch. On your worst days, we show up. When you're panicking and don't know what to do, we are there. What most people see, however, is the uniform and the badge, not the human being behind the badge. We are the people you pass in the grocery store, the ones you drive past on your way to work, the ones eating next to you at your favorite restaurant. We are just like you, we are human... but we are always there to help.

9

The Bizarre and Unusual

"Did you get an answer at the door?" Officer Suarez came up the steps of the front porch of the duplex as he asked me. He pulled up just as I knocked a second time.

"Not yet, no," I reply as I tap on the front window with the end of my flashlight. It was an abandoned call, meaning someone dialed 911 and then hung up. Abandoned calls make up a good chunk of what we respond to on the night shift. Most of the time, it's nothing, like a child playing with their parents' phone. But every abandoned call has to be checked out, just in case. Sometimes there's a domestic, and sometimes there's someone who seriously needs help. I knocked three times and didn't see or hear anything unusual coming from the house; it seemed like everything was in order. I got on the radio to ask dispatch if they could retry that phone number.

"Sorry it took me a while to get here," Suarez began. "I was over near the train stati..." Suarez didn't get a chance to finish as the sky lit up as bright as day. We both ducked down on the porch as if there was going to be an explosion or blast from something nearby. The sky went completely white for a second, the houses and streets lit up like it was daytime... and then went back to pitch black as if the light was just a memory. I stood there waiting for the sound of an explosion. I was absolutely sure something worse was coming. But it never came.

I have seen lightning strike close by. I've watched shooting stars light up the night sky for a split second. I had even witnessed a transformer catch fire, causing an electrical spark so bright that it lit up the surrounding parts of the city. But this was something I had never witnessed before in my life.

"What the hell was that?" I asked Suarez. I saw his wide-open eyes staring back at me. I was sure my eyes looked the same. We were both in shock.

"That was crazy," Suarez replied, looking around as if something on the street caused the city to become day for that short moment. I waited to hear some distant loud boom or explosion, but the street was silent. I expected people to come out from the neighboring houses to investigate, but no one came out. It was like Suarez and I were the only two people in the whole city to experience this bizarre event. I was glad Suarez was there and witnessed the strange, intensely bright light with me. No one would have believed me. We searched the area looking for the cause, but we didn't find anything. To this day, I still have no idea what that was.

Spooky, unusual, unexplained stories are my favorite stories to share with my family and friends, especially late at night. Every police officer I know seems to have a collection of weird, odd, and eerie stories... things they've encountered on the job... things that defy explanation. Have you ever noticed that after a "supernatural" event, the brain looks for logical scenarios to explain the phenomenon? It is as if we can't quite accept that something beyond our comprehension just happened. I know this doesn't seem to have any relevance to police work... or does it?

The dispatchers advised me that an elderly woman had called from the local hospital and appeared to be confused.

She gave her name – let's call her Bernadette Sanders – and told 911 operators that she didn't know where she was or how to get out. Our dispatchers advised me that they only knew where the call was coming from because it registered as a phone in the basement of our local hospital. Emergency dispatchers have access to this type of information to better locate people who need help. We've received these types of calls numerous times before, and it was usually a confused elderly person with dementia calling from a rehab or medical facility. I started towards the hospital. I planned to find this woman, put her at ease, and continue on with my night. I got to the hospital and talked to the woman at the front desk.

"I don't have any record of a Bernadette Sanders as a patient," she said.

"Okay, would I be able to check the basement? Apparently, she called from there."

"Sure," the nurse replied. "We can send the janitor down with you".

A janitor – who hadn't seen the light of day since 1996 but was apparently the only one with special access to the basement – escorted me down to the underbelly of the hospital but didn't stay. He obviously had other things to do and let me know that the elevator would take me back up when I was ready. Oh, and that there was likely no other living person down there at this hour. Great!

I've been in some creepy places in my life, but nothing compared to the hospital basement. It did not seem like part of the hospital; It felt like the basement of some old World War II bunker or a long-abandoned warehouse. The halls went on for more than a football field. One hallway had rusty pipes stretching towards some unknown room. The hallway got smaller and smaller, and it got hotter and muggier the further I went. So much so that I was sure I couldn't breathe in the air for long. I had to back out; it wasn't worth it. There was one last hallway I needed to check before I headed back up and called it a night. It was a normal-looking hallway until I turned the corner to the left. At that point, I saw a small-grade ramp turned up towards a pair of double doors. All of a sudden, I got that creepy feeling in my spine that I've felt all too often. Like I wasn't alone. Like I was being watched. I felt like I needed to leave right then.

I didn't need to know what was through those doors. I instinctively knew it was the morgue. I'm not sure why it hadn't occurred to me that the morgue would be in the basement. I made haste out of there.

On my way toward the exit of the hospital, I passed the front desk. The nurse I spoke with earlier stopped me on my way out.

"Oh, sir, that woman you asked for... Bernadette Sanders."

"Yes?" I said.

"She was a patient here... she died a few days ago."

While I was still in my first few years on the job, I got paired with the main man of the night shift, Jackson. He showed me the ropes in what would later be my main zone. Jackson was known to be very calm and relaxed in any situation, but he didn't put up with any nonsense. We answered a call regarding a woman screaming on the first floor of a duplex. But there's no one living on the first floor. Our caller said he lived on the second floor when we arrived; he had been waiting for us outside on the front porch.

"I keep hearing a girl screaming downstairs, but no one lives there. It's boarded up," he said to Jackson and me.

Jackson took the man's name and date of birth down and I followed the man inside. Thomas was his name. He was probably in his mid-thirties, of medium build. There was nothing noticeably odd about him at first glance.

"Merrick," Jackson said. "You go with him, and I'll see what I can find out around here." It didn't look like anyone lived in Thomas's apartment. He had no furniture. There was one room with lit candles, some snacks, a sleeping bag, and pages ripped out of a Bible and placed in an orderly fashion on the floor. Twenty minutes ago, I was enjoying a coffee while this guy was summoning portals to another dimension in a duplex in the hood. I moved on to the next room... I was already committed.

"How long have you lived here?" I tried to make small talk.

"Oh, about a month or so," I could tell.

Thomas led me to the back stairwell. We were up on the second floor and had to go back to the rear stairwell because, as he explained, all other doorways had been blocked off and boarded up as the first floor was vacated. However, he added that the only way to get to the first floor was to go all the way down to the basement and then up another set of stairs to the first floor. We started to walk down the two flights of stairs to the basement. He advised me that the door at the top of those stairs may also be barricaded. As we got to the basement and I realized that no light switches worked, I told Thomas to stay on the steps until I got back. I sensed that something was not adding up. I had my flashlight out and just enjoyed the creepy scenery for a moment. At the other end of the basement, I found the stairs leading up to the first floor. I started to climb the stairs and noticed that the door had been boarded up with nails. Then Jackson got me on the radio.

"Merrick, where are you?" he sounded unnerved.

"Inside... in the basement, trying to get to the first floor," I responded.

"Get out of there!" he all but shouted. "That guy doesn't even live here!"

If you ever get that moment where your uneasy feelings start to turn into reality, you know what I mean. I stopped on the stairs. I had the feeling that I was being watched. My hair stood up on my neck as I turned around to look down the stairs into the basement, shining my flashlight around. There at the bottom of the stairs was Thomas, his eyes lighting up from the shine of my flashlight like some rabid wolf. *I told him to stay put and he followed me.* I felt trapped. He heard everything Jackson said on the radio; it was time to go. Fear gripped me for a moment. I knew I had my gun, but this was some other fear. Thomas and I just looked at each other for a few seconds, waiting to see who was going to make the first move.

"I told you to stay on the stairs!" I shouted as I rushed toward him. I caught him by surprise. He stammered as if he was afraid of something, and I pushed him toward the back steps out of the basement. We were halfway up the stairs when I heard the loud scream of a woman coming from the steps where I had just been. But it didn't sound like it had come from the other side of the door; it sounded like it was right in the room with us. A deep chill shot up my spine and I came to a complete stop. Adrenaline rushed into my veins and I heard my heart beating in my ears. I was holding Thomas's shoulder – trying to push him further up the steps – so I felt him tense up, too.

"You heard it, right?" He trembled.

"Yes," I said. "But we are getting out of here right now."

Jackson and I searched the entire perimeter of the house after we secured Thomas in our car. Every window and door was boarded up. No one was inside. We called out; no one answered. We took Thomas to the homeless shelter after we grabbed his stuff from upstairs and blew out his candles. We never heard back from the landlord of the building. I will never know just what type of demonic shit this guy was doing in his apartment and if it caused the scream. The thing that gets me is that Thomas knew he was messing with powers he didn't understand. He may have caused the weird stuff that was going on in that place, yet it scared him so much that he needed to call the police. As far as I know, that house was renovated or sold. No one was ever found inside, and there was no evidence that anything unusual had happened inside, other than hearing that bizarre scream.

I had several calls about tripped motion alarms in homes where a family member had recently passed. *So, your motion alarm for your husband's study is going off for the first time in years, and your husband just passed away two nights ago*? A woman called 911, absolutely terrified because she saw a tall man in a suit walk through her house... and she lives alone. I've talked with many people who are delirious, on drugs, or sleep-deprived. This woman was not one of them; she was completely sane. She claimed she was watching T.V. in her living room when a man wearing a suit walked casually from her hallway, into the living room, and then to the kitchen. The woman quickly retrieved a BB gun that she had in her bedroom as she called the cops. She said she had the gun pointed at the man when we arrived, but that's when the man walked through the wall and was gone.

10

Fear and Loathing in a Pandemic

"How much contact did you have with the guy, though?" Lieutenant Grady was on the phone with one of the two officers who had just responded to an unresponsive young man who was pronounced deceased by the paramedics. It was later learned that he had died from a drug overdose – another big problem in the city –, but due to his age and the newly arrived Covid virus, we were taking full precautions. It was on everyone's minds at work that morning. *Was this our first case of Covid in the city?* I was at the station doing some paperwork from another call and could hear the lieutenant on the phone. "Okay, I'm going to have you and Levi bring your cars in and park them in the far lot near the gate. Once you have all of your stuff out of the vehicles, lock them up and head home... You don't need to come to the station for anything, do you?... Okay, good. Stay home and I'll call you to see if you need to go to urgent care for testing." Lieutenant Grady continued the conversation, but I didn't catch the rest. I was out the door and headed to my patrol vehicle to get back on my grid.

In the early part of 2020, there were rumors of the virus spreading. There was chaos in the cities and hospitals looked like war zones. After the first few Covid cases on American soil, we ramped up for a global pandemic that could disrupt everything we knew. Our department was already prepping for what was to come. All we knew was what the experts were telling us... and it sounded ominous. I began stockpiling water and canned goods, making mental plans for how I was going to safely get out of the city when society collapsed, reading up on water purification techniques and foraging like some crazed conspiracy theorist.

After the first few cases started to appear in our area, we knew it was only a matter of time before everyone caught the virus, too. As first responders, it is our job to be in contact with people every day. Try telling someone drunk and disorderly that they need to remain six feet from you and to keep their mask on. Even the intoxicated individuals who were not disorderly couldn't obey that rule. It would be like trying to run a day care and telling toddlers to keep in their seats and not put their fingers in their mouths... actually, that would be easier.

A few of my colleagues came down with Covid and were out sick for over a week. We got various reports back on how they were faring. "I feel fine, I just have a stuffy nose." "I have never been this sick in my life; this is worse than the flu." "I can breathe fine, but this awful headache will not go away." It seemed like the more we got into Covid season, the less we knew about the damn thing. The symptoms were... Everything.

Driving down the road and checking my computer screen for any calls in my zone, I noticed how dead the roads actually were. All of the bars and restaurants were closed. People were not going anywhere. If you ask most police officers how that time was on the job, they will tell you it was like Christmas. I'm certainly not trying to downplay the virus itself. I had a few people I was close with catch the virus, developed further complications, and passed from it. I'm just saying, for some people, that time was a much-needed vacation from social constraints.

My department conducted roll call outside now, instead of in our usual room at the station. They requested that all officers change into their work uniform at home and come in ready for work, so no one came into the station unless necessary. The funny thing was, however, there was a tiny hallway that we had to go through to get to our body cameras – it's only the most used hallway in the station. So everyone walked right next to each other anyway.

I started to feel like things were not as bad as we were being told when I walked into the hospital for a work call and saw some of the nurses not wearing their masks. They had their masks pulled down under their chin. Honestly, I don't blame them. I wouldn't be able to work well after twelve hours of breathing in my own exhaled air. I still crack up when I see people driving alone in their cars with their masks on.

We had Thanksgiving dinner at my mother's house during the pandemic. A week before, she needed to know exactly how many people were going to be coming for dinner, as the governor of our state mandated that only a certain number of people could attend a gathering at a time. There we were... all spaced out with our Thanksgiving plates of food. I cracked a joke about eating in the garage, but no one thought it was funny. We had the curtains drawn shut because we expected the governor to pay a surprise visit to do a head count that day.

A good percentage of my department had already taken sick leave because of Covid. It was coming up on a year, and I still hadn't caught it. I was a little jealous because I really needed a few days off to catch up on some things. Then one night, I felt a little off. It wasn't a feeling of coming down with something, or feeling sick, I just felt like my brain was.... Going slow. The gamble at the end of the shift was whether or not I should get tested at the urgent care. I could be there all morning. If I were negative for Covid, then I would have wasted all that time and missed out on sleep. I decided to take the chance and drove on over.

The nurse at the clinic got me in before too long. "Do you feel sick or have you been in contact with anyone who has Covid?" the nurse asked as she inserted a long Q-tip up my nose. I tried not to move my head to prevent my brain from being poked.

"Well, I have constant contact with people for my job, so I'm not sure about exposure. But I just feel off."

"We will know the results in a few minutes," she said as she took the second Q-tip from my nostril and put it in a small bag. My nose itched like crazy.

I had a moment of prayer while I was sitting there waiting for my test results. The nurse came back sooner than expected. "I have some bad news, Mr. Merrick," she began. I thought, *Shit, I'm not getting those days off.*

"Negative?" I replied.

"No," she looked confused. "I'm sorry, but it came back positive." She must have seen a slight smile on my face that I thought I was hiding. "Did... did you want this to come back positive?" she asked.

"Yes, I'm sorry. I don't mean to be insensitive... But I just really needed a few days off."

The nurse handed me my papers with my test results later, and I ran out of the clinic holding that paper like Charlie with his Golden Ticket. Don't read me wrong, I'm not one to abuse sick time, I actually didn't use one sick day my first five years on the job. Planned vacation is one thing, but when you get an unexpected week off – no plans, no obligations, no social expectations. It is the best mental health break you could ask for. I spent all week catching up on things I hadn't had time for the past few years –

cleaned and organized, read some books, worked out every day, and made healthy meals. And I was entirely fortunate that I never felt sick.

Back on the streets, it was business as usual. I'm convinced some people didn't even know we were in a pandemic. I still saw the same individuals walking around picking cigarette butts up off the ground to get just enough tobacco to roll a McGyver-style, makeshift cigarette. They had no fear of Covid, or any virus for that matter – and they didn't seem to get sick! Who were these people who barely needed to eat, sleep, or drink fresh water? They could sleep outside in near-freezing temperatures, get up, shrug it all off, and wander around the rest of the day. Even though there are shelters and rehabilitation programs within a short walk.

When things finally went back to normal, businesses started to reopen, and people began to socially gather again. Streets seemed littered with masks that had been carelessly discarded, but the garbage eventually found its way to the trash. And the calls started to come in again; we were back to full service.

11

The Good With the Bad

Grand Theft Auto

Years later, I was just about to park my patrol car for a bit near one of the busier roads of my zone. The sergeant on my shift got on the radio to advise everyone that he was at the gas station and had eyes on a stolen vehicle that was reported earlier that night. It was one of those warm sunny mornings... the sun had just come up an hour ago and there was fresh dew on the grass. Traffic wasn't that congested in the city yet. Moments later, the sergeant radioed that he tried to stop the sedan, but it took off at a high rate of speed east on the parkway. That's the road

I was parked near, and I realized the vehicle was heading right my way. I heard my sergeant report that the vehicle was going close to ninety miles per hour and that he was slowing down to prevent an accident. The parkway itself is about two miles long and, at that speed, I figured the vehicle was about to crest the hill and I'd have eyes on it. I pull out from the parking spot I'm at and start eastbound.

I thought about blocking the road, but then realized that was an awful idea, as that would surely lead to an accident. As I looked ahead, I saw two cars just reach the red light at the intersection one hundred yards from me. Just in time to see the car thief crest the hill behind me, I flicked on my emergency lights, hoping the drivers ahead of me would see and get out of the way. They didn't. The stolen sedan flew by me at a phenomenal speed, with nowhere to go up ahead because those two cars took up the two lanes. I followed in pursuit. There was about five feet between the two stopped cars and this criminal seemed to think he could pass right between them! A second later, the car smashed in between the two stopped cars and spread them apart like a bouncer cutting through a crowd. It was absolute carnage as debris scattered all over the road after the loud noise of metal smashing together. I assumed the car thief would be out of commission after that because most of them don't wear seatbelts, but the car kept rolling and turned into traffic at the intersection.

I saw three or four other vehicles approach the intersection from the other side and the sedan was headed for them. That's when I noticed the driver was hanging half out of the driver's side window. I wasn't sure if he was hanging out because he had been almost thrown out after the crash or if he was trying to escape. I passed quickly between the two damaged cars just as the sergeant had pulled up. I knew other units were on their way and would be able to check with the victims of the crash. I focused on the approaching traffic and stopping this nitwit.

There was a small hill below the roadway and some houses beyond that. The rolling car continued on as I saw the driver trying to pull himself out of the window. The car was about to go down the hill and the driver was about to be cut in half by a tree! Just in time, he rolled out of the vehicle and onto the grass. The car came to a halt in the grass and got stuck. Within a second, the driver was up and running for the houses. I parked my car right in traffic and immediately fled after him. The chase went through several yards as I continued to gain on him. Many people have run from me throughout the years; many people are faster than me. But few have my endurance. I can keep a good pace for miles.

House after house and yard after yard, I broke out from the rear of one house just in time to see him go behind another. I could tell I was getting closer and I anticipated he would stop behind one of the houses to try to get a jump on me, but I was ready to give him my all. At this point, I had no idea where I was or what street I was on. If I had to call out with my location for my fellow officers or dispatch, I wouldn't even be able to. We had to be coming to a familiar street soon. I broke through to the next rear yard and saw him switch direction to try to lose me. As he got close to a fence, he attempted to jump it, but he slipped on the dewy grass and smacked his face right on the wooden edges of the fence. I think I either winced or laughed because I knew how much that must have hurt. He made the fence, and I was right behind him, making sure not to make the same mistake he did. I jumped over the fence and was just feet from his heels when we ran down a driveway and out to the road.

He stopped on the front lawn of the house and turned around with his hands up like he was ready to fight. He knew he couldn't outrun me now, so this was his last resort.

I could see he was winded and wouldn't beat me in this fight. Instead of punching him, I tackled him to the ground. He started to give up and I managed to get him on his stomach and almost had handcuffs on him. My sergeant, who had been driving the streets looking for us, found us. He slammed on the brakes and was out of the car in a split second to help me handcuff the guy, who was now swinging his arms. Once we had his arms pinned down, the man could only move his head. I just got the cuffs on him when he moved his face over to the sergeant's ankle and took a solid bite. The sergeant yelled, *"You freaking bit me!"* There were some more expletive words used, but you can figure them out.

The criminal was arrested and charged with everything that he could be charged with. The owner of the stolen vehicle came to reclaim some of his property before the tow truck came to get his totaled car. And the victims of the crash were treated for non-life-threatening injuries. The only person who had to go through hell after this incident was the sergeant. He had to get numerous inoculations to treat the bite since we had no idea what that man had in his system. Fight if you must fight us, run if you must run. Just don't bite or spit.

The Girl in the Penguin Costume

Early on in my career, I worked many nights in the booking office – more than I'd care to recall. It's one thing to deal with the unruly on the streets – I could get them placed somewhere and be rid of them, then go about my business. It's another thing to have to babysit them all night in booking. Even though I've had countless nonstop nights on the street filled with paperwork, calls, arguing, and yelling, nothing drains me more than being stuck in the booking office dealing with one person who just can't stop asking questions or making noise.

It was just before midnight when I entered the booking office. I was told there was only one prisoner on the bench. I stepped in to find one female prisoner cuffed to the bench... wearing a penguin costume. The worst part was that she spoke no English. I can't remember what she was charged with, just that she was young – not older than twenty – and wore that penguin costume all night. Back then, we had a female matron, Lorraine, who assisted with any female prisoners. She just started her shift for the night. She came into my office and closed the door behind her.

"Merrick," she looked puzzled, "why is she dressed like a penguin?"

"She was protesting global warming, Lorraine."

I wasn't in court that morning as the girl went before a judge, but I can only gather that she stepped into that courtroom still wearing that penguin costume.

The Pez Dispenser

On one such booking night, I sat in the office, just tidying up some paperwork, when three officers brought in a very colorful character. The man was short and wiry with some long, crazy hair – think Sideshow Bob. He wore a t-shirt and gym shorts and spoke Spanish to people who weren't there. The cops suspected he was holding onto drugs... somewhere other than his pockets.

I had become friends with one of the sergeants on the night shift, Sergeant Johnson. In fact, Johnson and I remained friends after his retirement and still catch up when we both have a day off. Sergeant Johnson was one of those funny guys who always had a joke about everything. Every workplace has one – the person everyone enjoys working with because you know you will have some laughs. As fun as he was, I learned not to upset Sergeant Johnson. He had a long fuse, but if you got on his bad side, you'd see someone else. On this night, Johnson guided this wild character towards the booking bench.

"He's got some drugs in him, I think," Johnson said as he shook the man's hips. One small bag of narcotics fell out of the guy's shorts and onto the floor. He looked up at Johnson and then at me as if he was amazed his rectum was hiding things from him. Johnson gave him another good shake, and another bag of narcotics fell out. "He's a freaking Pez dispenser," Johnson exclaimed, before I fell back into the booking office, trying not to cry while I was laughing. The man was booked on his narcotics possession charges once he was thoroughly shaken out.

Dementia and a Kitchen Knife

Some people have weapons and intend to use them. Some are not in their right minds. Some just need a calm voice to talk to. I was riding with a new officer on a colder night and things seemed to be pretty average. We responded to a call from a panicked son who was caring for his dad, who suffered from dementia. The father awoke and found his son in the house, but didn't recognize him and mistook him for an intruder. The father pulled out a long kitchen knife and chased his son around the house. When we pulled up, the man's other son had met us in the parking lot. He was almost crying – he was worried his dad was going to stab his brother inside, but mostly because he was worried that the police would shoot his dad if he didn't put the knife away. I assured him that no one was getting hurt tonight.

We made our way through the rear patio to the back door and knocked. Luckily, the lights were all on inside, so I could see into the house. A man in his seventies cautiously started towards the door with the large knife clenched in his hand. I could see the frightened son further in the kitchen. As a precaution, my partner and I had our guns drawn but held low. I announced to the man who came to the door who I was and to drop the knife. Anger showed in his eyes, and he seemed confused. He held the knife up and shouted for us to get out of his house. I had the rear door open slightly, but could see him through the windowpane. He continued to walk toward us with the knife held up. I realized he didn't understand the situation, so I tried a different approach. Maybe scaring him would work.

I forcefully opened the door and yelled at him to put the knife down. He could now see my gun in my hand; now he appeared to understand that we were there as police officers.

The man crept back towards the kitchen table. He paused a few times as he was hesitant to put the knife down. I yelled again for him to drop it on the table, then calmly told him we were there to help him. The man put the knife down and stepped back again. Immediately, I grabbed the knife from the table. I told him to have a seat and assured him he was safe and we would help him. I handed the knife to his son behind me, and we continued to talk. The man still didn't recognize his sons and insisted that one of them had broken into his house. I told him that they were good people who were there to help. He was not in any danger. We told the sons to hide the knives in the house, then our job was done. It stuck with me, though... because of the dementia, the man couldn't recognize his own son's face, but he could still recognize the police uniform.

The Deer and the Blanket

One cold, winter night, while I was still on field training, we responded to a car/deer accident. I was riding with a friendly sergeant who was a spitfire when she needed to be. We arrived at the accident and found the young deer in the roadway, sadly with two broken legs. This was my first time on an accident like this, so it was a learning experience. The sergeant called another officer to the scene to dispatch the deer once the roadway was closed off. It's a sad but humane way to stop the animal from suffering.

The sergeant and the other officer spoke with the driver and directed him down the road to a parking lot to get his report when they were done. I was not far up the street in my jacket, standing near the patrol car directing traffic down another road. As I stood outside, a nice woman came out of her house. Her doorway was off to the side of the house, so she didn't have a view of the deer. She stayed on her step, probably because it was too cold for her to step all the way outside.

"Is everything okay?" she asks nervously.

"Oh yes, ma'am," I replied. "Just an accident with a deer." I manage not to give out too much information.

"Oh goodness! Is everyone okay?" she asks.

"Yes, everyone is good. The deer is injured pretty badly, though." At this point, I wasn't sure if she was more concerned about the deer or the driver. At this, the woman goes back inside, and I figured that was the last I would see of her.

The sergeant got on the radio and advised our dispatchers that any shots-fired calls in the area would more than likely be them. I know at this point the deer is about to be shot and we will be back in the warm car shortly. A minute passes. The nice woman opens her side door and steps out with a nice wool blanket.

"Officer, this is for the deer if it's too co..." I imagine she was going to finish with the word "cold," but she didn't get the chance to finish. The loud BOOM made the woman and me both jump. It was quiet for a few seconds before I responded, seeing the confused look in her eyes.

"Thank you, miss, I don't think the deer will need it, though."

Just One More Thing

For a structure fire, our protocol is to block traffic and hold the area down for the firefighters to do their job. Many times, we arrive on the fire scene first, thus causing a dilemma. Do we leave our patrol vehicles to ensure everyone is out of the house? Or do we stick to protocol and control traffic on the road? I always say, human lives are more important than protocol.

Early one morning, I was right around the corner from a reported structure fire in my zone. When I pulled up, smoke was already billowing out of an attic window of this two-floor home. A large number of people were outside, standing under the roof of their porch adjacent to the house. I jumped out of my car and yelled at the family to get away from the house. They lazily strolled towards their side yard near some vehicles, as I asked if anyone else was in the house. A scared woman replied that her husband was still up on the second floor. I panicked because, in my mind, no sane person would willingly stay in there. He must have passed out from the smoke, I thought. I ran to the side door and up the stairs, holding my hand over my mouth from the smoke and fumes.

I had to pause in the second-floor living room for a moment as I tried to make out what I was seeing. There was a large hole in the middle of the ceiling and the whirl of flames flowing up into the attic created a sort of vortex of flame and smoke. Whatever was burning caused something to drip bright drops of molten plastic or metal down through the hole and onto the floor. I shouted for anyone who was still inside. I hoped that the man was still conscious, so I could find him and get him out before we both die. I heard no answer. I called out again, and this time, I heard the guy yelling back from a side room at the other end of the house. Part of me was amazed he answered. The other part of me wondered why he was still in the burning house. Maybe he was trying to find a pet.

I cautiously ran around the burning hole in the ceiling, praying that the whole thing wouldn't come down on my head, and found the man in the back room grabbing items. He had a VR headset in his hand and was looking around through clothes.

"What the hell are you doing, man?" I yelled. "We have to get out of here!"

"Okay, okay," he replied. I had him follow me around the fiery hole in the living room and run down the steps to get fresh air. Outside, I saw the family had only moved ten feet and were congregating around their vehicles. I shouted at them to get across the street. What is wrong with this family, I thought. I almost fell backwards as I looked behind me and the man was nowhere in sight. He must still be upstairs.

Sirens sounded as firefighters arrived just as I ran back up the stairs towards the death trap. I located the man in another room, stacking clothes hastily from his closet onto a bed. "Are you freaking kidding me?" I yelled at him. "We are going now, if I have to drag you out." This time, I made sure he was in front of me as we went down the stairs. The firefighters met us at the doorway and looked at the man with his arms full of his stuff. "Seriously?" one of them muttered as they continued past us and up the stairs.

Later, I got briefed about not going into burning buildings and how my job is to keep traffic blocked for the fire department. I took that under advisement.

Bomb Squad

Last-minute calls at the end of your shift often mean you are not leaving work on time. This can throw off your day, especially if you have plans or errands to run after work. Suspicious package calls almost always come in the morning. This one came in about fifteen minutes before the end of my shift and I groaned. I had way too much to do to get stuck on this call. According to dispatch, someone saw a suspicious man walk up to a local building in our city. The caller said the man set a briefcase down along the side of the building and walked away.

I showed up a few moments later and spotted a black briefcase propped up against the side of the building, just as the caller described. Not a common sight, and it was even more suspicious that someone just set it down and walked away. I called over a senior officer, Robert, who was working the next zone over and asked him to witness the event should anything happen. Robert started to protest a bit. Apparently, this abandoned briefcase was an unusual sight to him as well. But I had a good feeling that this was not that type of suspicious package and that it was just a coincidence that someone had left a briefcase here. Approaching the case, I carefully picked it up and moved it towards the sidewalk, making sure no one else was around. I had Robert stand near his patrol car just in case. The briefcase was light, so I set it down and examined it a bit closer. The thing wasn't ticking and didn't appear to have any wires coming out of it.

"I'm going to open it now," I called out to Robert. I didn't have time to look at him; I just focused on the briefcase. Carefully, I slid back each latch as they snapped with a low click. So far, so good. I was ready for anything at this point. I just opened it to end the suspense and anxiety.

Empty.

I felt a release of adrenaline. Just an old tattered briefcase. I threw the thing in my car to dispose of it on the way into the police station. Robert looked at me as I walked back towards our vehicles. "You're crazy," he said, as we called it a day.

Cat calls

Sometimes the saddest beginnings can have a funny ending. You never know how an incident will end up. It was a perfect, sunny morning and I was all set to leave work for the day. The day shift was short-staffed, and I got the call that I was being held over until noon. The gorgeous sunshine had me feeling energized, so I didn't mind working the extra four hours that morning. I grabbed a coffee and prepared to cruise around to pass the time until the first call came in.

It was just after 8 am when I got the call for my zone about a cat that had just been hit by a truck. The cat's owners had called and advised that they didn't think the cat would make it. I can deal with almost anything at work, but seeing animals suffer is one thing that really bothers me. I dreaded what I was about to deal with, but I started to the address on Gould Street to see what could be done, praying that the cat would pass before I got there. It did not.

The cat was struggling when I got there, lying right at the edge of the road. I could smell skunk when I pulled up. The man who called me met me on the sidewalk. He explained that the cat was more like a stray that they had been feeding. They didn't know what else to do but call the police. I asked the man if he had a blanket for the cat because I, at the very least, wanted the poor thing to be comfortable as it passed. It was not going to make the quick trip to the local vet. I stayed with the cat, lightly petting it as it went. It pained me, but I was glad the suffering was done. The whole time, I couldn't get that skunk smell out of my nostrils. I looked up the street to see that the skunk may have been hit by the same truck. I spotted the dead skunk in the road, only about four houses away.

The man was now standing outside with his daughter. I asked them if they wanted to bury the stray. They did not. I was not sure what to do next – it was still my first year on the job. I knew that we transported deceased dogs to a local animal shelter, but I wasn't sure if we did the same for cats. I called the sergeant on the street.

"Have you been on that call long enough, Merrick?" Sergeant Whitney asked as he answered the phone.

"The cat didn't make it, sir," I responded, as if I was going to get sympathy for the stray. "The owner," I sort of lied a bit, but I didn't want to go into details about how the man had been feeding a stray, but didn't have an emotional connection to the cat, "is here and doesn't want to bury it. I'm not sure what to do with it."

"Well, if it's their pet and they can't take it, we need to bring it up to the humane society. You should have a black plastic bag in your trunk." I fumbled around in the trunk, looking for the bag, but couldn't find one. There was a slight sigh on the phone from Sergeant Whitney.

"Okay, I'm at the station and have one here," he said. "I'll bring it to you. You're at 504 Gould Street, right?"

"Yes, sir, thank you," I hung up.

I stood there for a few minutes with the man and his daughter, not able to shake that skunk smell from up the street. Then I came up with the most wonderful idea.

"Sir, my sergeant is on his way here to pick up the cat." I started.

"Yes," he already knew.

"Do you mind stepping down with me to that house over there and standing with me in front of that skunk?" I asked. "I have an idea."

I could see that he was already working out where I was going with this, and to my amazement, he agreed happily. The man followed me down the road after I had set the cat carefully on the lawn, wrapped in the blanket. The only thing visible in the road was the plump, odiferous skunk.

What I didn't realize was that the guy's little daughter followed us down as well and was willing to play in the prank.

Fifteen minutes had passed, and I was worried that maybe Sergeant Whitney had played the joke on me and no bag was coming. After all, he did say I was taking way too long on this call already and he probably didn't care for cats as much as I did. Just then, I saw the sergeant's patrol vehicle come around the corner. The three of us stood on the side of the road in front of this dead skunk.

The sergeant pulls up with his windows down as I step up to his vehicle. He didn't even look at me. He just stared straight ahead at the motionless white and black object in the street that clearly was not a striped cat. "Merrick, that's a freaking skunk!"

"No, sir," I reply, struggling to keep a smile from creeping up my face. "That's this guy's cat. They saw it get hit this morning after they fed it."

"Yes, sir, that's my cat. Got hit by a truck this morning," the guy added, without me having to even ask.

Sergeant Whitney looked intently at the skunk through his window, trying to puzzle it out. "Okay then," was all he said as he pulled on some rubber gloves and grabbed the plastic bag from the front seat. He then steps out of his patrol vehicle as I try my hardest not to let him hear me laughing. Luckily, he did not.

Sergeant Whitney approached the dead animal and got a closer look at it. He went quiet for a few seconds, then shouted, "MERRICK, THIS IS A FREAKING SKUNK!"

The man, his daughter, and I busted up laughing, and the sergeant joined in. I think it was the first time I cried while laughing on this job.

"Was there even a cat?" he asked. I showed him where the actual cat was and assured him that this whole call was not a prank. I remember leaving work that day a little more comfortable with the job, knowing that even in the bad times, good can come out of it. Sergeant Whitney and I still joke about that morning to this day.

12

A Theory on Crime

Off the clock and out of uniform, Sergeant Johnson and I were sitting at the local gas station and coffee shop, conversing with the locals. At this time in my life, I had no wife or pets to get home to, so we took our time to unwind and have some laughs. The employees of the shop didn't mind us hanging around, as we were recognized by a lot of the regulars and would deter a lot of their usual nonsense, such as petty theft. We had our usual table with our usual crew, sipping coffee and catching up on the latest local news.

During the morning hours, we would see familiar faces from the night before, stumbling in to use the ATM or begging for money outside. They had been up all night, and so had we, but we were getting a paycheck. The number of people who wander around all night is almost unbelievable, especially to those who haven't seen it for themselves. I knew the services that were offered in this city for homelessness, drug rehabilitation, and mental health crises. Yet, the people we dealt with, a majority of the time, do not want any help.

It still amazes me how people can be content living in apartments filled with trash, sleeping on blankets or towels draped over garbage, because they just don't feel like cleaning up. I can't fathom people who choose to sleep outside and look for drugs instead of a warm bed in the winter, or people who stand all day on the street corners with signs saying that they are homeless and need money for their families... individuals who I know don't have families that they need to provide for.

How did we get here? And where are we going?

This is the point where I would like to outline my theory of diet and crime correlation, but first, I'd like to paint a picture.

It's another morning and the parents are up and rushing to get ready for work. A classic, traditional, two-parent household. The biggest struggle of the morning is getting the kids up and ready for school. They are very tired and have been up most of the night, unable to sleep well. Television screens and smartphones are never far from their reach and the blue light is what keeps them up way too late. Time seems to fly and it's past midnight before the kids even realize it. There is now no time for a healthy breakfast to start the day. So the parents tell the kids to grab something to eat quickly before the bus comes. If there is a little time, they might have a bowl of cereal, toaster pastries, a muffin, or maybe a cup of yogurt. Don't forget the milk. If there is no time, they settle for a cereal bar that can be eaten on the way or nothing at all. The brain gets its quick fix, like a junkie who needs a little something to feel normal, to function, for an hour.

Now the kids have a stomach full of sugar, empty carbs, and dairy. And don't forget the BHT and other harmful preservatives. BHT (butylated hydroxytoluene) is a common ingredient added to processed foods to keep them from going bad and extend shelf life. While approved in small amounts, it has raised concerns because some studies suggest it may disrupt hormones and potentially contribute to long-term health risks with long-term exposure.

School starts and the crash begins around the second period. Now there seems to be no fuel left, little energy to stay awake and even less to focus and pay attention to what is being taught. Luckily, lunch is around the corner, but what is being served for lunch in most American lunchrooms? Pizza and deli meat sandwiches containing Nitrites and Nitrates. Most school lunches are carbohydrate-heavy with added cheese. There are very few lunch options with fresh, non-chemical-laden vegetables. If there is a side salad, it is small and contains one carrot that looks like it was found under the fridge after a month. Instead of providing a full meal of nutritious foods, school lunches simply give the kids another quick fix... enough energy to get through another class, maybe two. Cue the behavioral issues and irritability. Are students with ADHD and autism struggling at this time the most? Do they need a trip to the nurse's office to get medication that has been left for them just for this purpose?

The school day has ended and the kids are on their way home. It is now either time to nap or get energized with some screen time – television, video games, or jumping on their tablet or computer. The class work that couldn't be completed in class because of a lack of energy and motivation is still waiting to be done. But now it's time to relax, they think. After all, they've already put in a full day at school.

Dinner time is our best chance of steering the ship back towards a healthy medium. But now the parents are home from work and drained from their hectic day. What's quick and easy? A frozen pizza, pasta and a side, or ordering out. Everyone eats together and now it's time to tie up loose ends from the day, so the cycle can start over again tomorrow.

This is just an example of a normal household. If we looked at the single-parent families and those living in poverty, I assure you, it's much worse. Poor nutrition is only part of the problem. Kids spend too much time on social media, where they see people being rewarded for doing dumb things for views and fame. Our kids are being taught the basics in school to get them to college, which they may or may not attend. And that's if they do well. The fundamentals of life are left to be taught by the parents, if they aren't too busy with what they have to do.

So, now we have generations of parents in our cities who are almost nonexistent in the home and in their kids' lives. Children are raising themselves, and usually the wrong way. Mental health deteriorates and the motivation is virtually nonexistent. The influences on kids' lives are their friends, who are in the same boat as they are. If kids do manage to pull themselves away from in front of the T.V. or smartphone to go outside, they spend it wandering around the streets. What's a few broken windows? Or taking some things out of cars? No one cares anyway. When those petty crimes stop giving them an adrenaline boost, it's time to graduate to stealing an item from the local convenience store. No one got caught the first time, and it felt good to get something for free. And if they are caught, it's a slap on the wrist, totally worth it.

Like sugar and caffeine, stealing gives the brain a temporary feel-good boost that kids want to replicate over and over again. This is how the cycle of addiction starts. When the action no longer gives them the same boost, it is time to try new things. Someone offers a cigarette, an alcoholic drink, or a joint. Then smoking and drinking become daily habits. The friends are the new family. The kid is starting to feel good and accepted in ways they don't get at home. In the cities, this is a major reason why younger people get involved with gangs. The teenager or young adult gets acceptance and a sense of belonging to something greater. The cigarettes and booze give way to harder drugs. They no longer break windows. Jumping people for money doesn't seem so bad. Stealing from houses and stealing cars is looked on by the group or gang with admiration. The streets are dangerous, and people have guns. The teenager no longer wants to carry a knife. Where can we get a gun? Most of the shootings I've been on were carried out by someone younger than twenty. The next age group is people in their mid-twenties or younger.

So, now we are at the forefront of the issues. If the individual isn't shot or incarcerated, they have an addiction and severe mental health issues by the time they reach their twenties. I wish I could say that only a small percentage of people follow this path, but that is not the case. Without a positive intervention on the part of caring parents or a positive influence in their lives, it is the way a lot of children will go. The teenager and young adult may try their hand at a career or job, but where will the motivation to continue working be when their minimum-wage paychecks start coming in and they realize it is not enough to live on? Only the highly motivated and highly educated are guaranteed to make it... and even that isn't really guaranteed. You can probably think of a handful of people you know who are working full-time and still just trying to get by, people who haven't done anything wrong in their lives.

It is possible to stop the cycle before it even begins. It starts with a proper diet and positive reinforcement, and it starts at an early age. Our brains require a certain amount of vitamins and minerals every day, and our bodies are the same. It is not easy. Even the healthiest person may struggle to consume all the recommended nutrients he or she needs every day. That is where the discipline comes into play. If we continue on a diet of empty carbohydrates, sugar, sodas, dairy, with very few fresh vegetables, our mental health will continue to decline.

Mental health decline starts at such a slow, steady pace that the individual can't see it. When I worked in the homeless shelter, I saw it over time. I had clients coming in off the street every six months, almost acting like entirely different people, like zombies. And then, while working as a cop, I saw the same people, completely devoid of intellectual thought. People I talked with late into the night when I had met them at the shelter are now, almost twenty years later, like empty husks.

Meals of carbs and sugar in the morning lead to attention disorders as well as addiction and behavioral issues that get progressively worse with each passing year. A corrupt mind will not be able to make sound decisions when it comes to food, friendships, the future, and the issues will have a snowball effect. Gang crime leads to gun violence and homicides. Individual addictions lead to overdoses and deaths. Minor mental health issues lead to greater mental health issues that tend towards suicide and homicide.

A child backed by the right nutrition will have the mental fortitude to make the right decisions with a sound mind. A child with the right foods may have the energy and motivation needed to step outside of the local norm, dream big, and turn from negative friends.

It starts with diet. It starts at a young age. It starts with the individual. Our duty as parents, as community members, as adults, is to steer the minds of our youths back on the right track so they can think for themselves and motivate themselves. Mistakes will be made... life happens. But the well-equipped mind can overcome anything.

So how do we steer the ship back in the right direction? I would not be so foolish as to believe that we could change the diets at home and at school and expect a significant drop in the crime rates across the board. No, there are numerous factors that go into fixing the day-to-day issues that we all face in our community. A trend I have witnessed, however, is that a lot of the home issues stem from children raising children. If the adult does not act responsibly and take care of themselves, they are not going to properly be able to take care of their kids. That leaves us with teachers, police officers, counselors, and older family members bearing the burden. As children, we have that sense of security growing up that the adults are in control and we are safe. We get older and realize that not every adult who is in charge is trustworthy and responsible. Hence, the adolescent's distrust of authority figures. Now, imagine you are a first responder and the world seems to be only children wearing adult clothes, making poor decisions guided by emotion. I exaggerate obviously, but I'm only trying to paint a picture. We can take the right steps forward as a community by continuing to help these children, and individually by being the best versions of ourselves. The only unfortunate thing I realize is that the ones who need to read this will more than likely not.

In addition to sharing some wild stories and experiences from my life on the grid, my goal is to start a conversation about the underlying social issues that contribute to crime, mental illness, homelessness, addiction, and other problems every police department and every community deals with. I've incorporated what I've learned about nutrition, mental health, and how they relate to many of the issues we face in America. What stands out is the sharp contrast between severe mental illness and exceptional mental strength. Yet our attention is almost entirely on what's wrong – diagnosing, labeling, and fixing.

We rarely turn our focus to those who are thriving mentally and emotionally and ask how they got there. There is something to be learned from them. In my view, much of that difference comes down to motivation and discipline.

13

Day One

Field training day one, hour one.

My scheduled field training officer had taken our first day off, so I was placed with another FTO, Carl. Carl was the type of officer everyone looked up to. He's old-school and had a joke for just about everything. For him, the name of the game was put your time in, get to the end of the day, go home, forget about work. So, I really couldn't have had a better first day.

"First rule," Carl started in. "We do rounds of our zone for the first hour, no stopping for coffee." I nodded my head as he looked over at me. He put the car in drive and we headed out of the police station lot. "But we gotta get some coffee," he added with a smile.

So, our first stop was getting coffee. A quick pass through the drive-thru and we were back on the road. We had a relatively easy yet large zone to cover. It was the southern part of the city, mostly residential and with businesses. The nicer houses were closer to the southern edge of the city and there were lots of winding roads up into the hills. I was all decked out in way too much gear, and my work pack was crammed with everything I thought I would need. Most shifts, all I ever needed was a pad of paper and a pen.

We weren't out on the street long for our tour when the calls started coming in – vehicle larcenies on the south side. All on one street. I remember thinking how crazy that was for my first day. Later, I realized that's business as usual for degenerates who have nothing better to do at night but break into cars. We set off for the first call and to speak with the first victim, a nice businessman living in a quaint house on a side street. The first week was supposed to be just observation, and, to be honest, I was relieved because I wouldn't have even known where to begin. The back window of the man's car was busted out and some change was stolen from inside. Ridiculous. That amount of damage for some loose pocket change. Carl took the information down as I soaked everything in. A few hours later, we finished taking reports for all the larcenies on that street, and we went back to cruising around.

Lunchtime came before I knew it. We stopped at a nice little Italian deli that sold sandwiches and other homemade items. A few of the daytime officers stopped in to join us and I felt like a little kid again. I was having trouble taking off my jacket with the radio cord wrapped around me. I must have looked foolish in that oversized winter jacket when it was well above thirty degrees outside and the sun was shining. Putting my jacket in the trunk was the best decision I made that day. After lunch, Carl let me drive the car even though I was only supposed to be observing, and he made a good point. "You went through all that training; you know how to drive the cars. Why would I not have you drive the car now?"

Carl told me to park at the corner of a side street along one of the busier roads to see if we could stop any vehicles. I noticed a man talking on his cell phone, so we followed him and hit the lights. The driver promptly stopped. Carl looked up the plate number while I made contact with the guy. My first stop!

As I approached the car, I could see a badge in the driver's hand. It was another cop. He had explained how he was on the phone with his supervisor, trying to resolve an issue. I looked over at Carl, who was still in the car. When he looked up and saw me, he knew there was an issue and came out. Carl couldn't believe that on my very first traffic stop, I pulled over another cop! Prior to making the stop, Carl and I decided we weren't going to write a ticket for that stop because it was just to give me experience. We continued on with our day.

Two hours before my first day came to a close, a call came out for a larceny at the local grocery store in our zone. We were just around the corner. Dispatch advised us that a female had taken items and was preparing to leave the store. We caught her at the front door as soon as we pulled up. She knew she was busted and didn't resist. It was easy to handcuff her, place her in the back of our patrol car, and start typing up the larceny charge. Carl showed me how to type up the charge, which was relatively easy. He had a way of making things look simple, and he always said repetition was the best teacher for the job. While he was explaining how to print out the charge, the girl in the back leaned forward, interested.

"Oh!" she exclaimed, "Are you training?" She seemed genuinely intrigued.

"Yeah," I laugh. "First day."

"Really? That's great, you're doing a good job," she added. Part of me was worried I would get in trouble for conversing with someone we just arrested, but Carl thought it was a funny remark as well.

"Thank you," I said. "Although I have a lot more to learn."

"You'll get there," she said in an encouraging way as she sat back in the seat. Amazing, I thought. I'm getting advice and well-wishes from my first arrest.

We finished the charge and had the store employee sign it. Then we drove back to the police station to have the girl booked on her larceny charge. It's a relatively quick process – she was out in time for family dinner, if that's where she was headed. On her way out the door, she turned to me and said, "You're doing a great job. Keep up the good work."

My first day as a police officer couldn't get any better. The next few months, however, were a crude awakening.

End Notes

I had three main goals for writing this book: to encourage people who want to become a police officer but are unsure of the process or doubt their own abilities; to support current officers who may be struggling, feeling burnt out, or having trouble seeing the good they are doing amid all the chaos; and lastly, to educate the public about the issues officers face every day, mostly with onslaught of mental health calls and domestic issues.

I know that my ten years in this career may seem, to some, to be too short to write a book. I have read other books written by retired police officers, books I still enjoy to this day. But something led me to write this book... and to write it now. Maybe I will write another book after I've logged another ten years on the force. If you are reading this book, and it's after midnight, chances are good that I'm out there somewhere... possibly washing green slime off my uniform so I can get back to my grid.

I wrote this book now and not later because tomorrow is not promised. I still consider myself new in my understanding of nutrition, mental illness, addiction, and life. I have a lot more to endure, experience, observe, and learn. In the last four years, however, I've noticed a change in the volume and types of calls I respond to as a police officer. Mental health issues seem to be at an all-time high. Emotionally disturbed persons are causing more issues with the public and with first responders. Damages, injuries, and social strain caused by subjects who are not emotionally or mentally stable have been on the increase. And although we have numerous resources and programs to help these individuals, the ones who do need the help are not seeking it.

So why write this book? Why share these stories? Life can and will take some unexpected turns. When I was riding a stolen steamroller down the street years ago, I never thought I would one day be a police officer stopping other misguided youths from pulling dangerous pranks. Strength does not just come from perseverance, resilience, and inner resolve. True strength comes from forgiveness, or so I believe. Conflict is inevitable. Of trials and challenges in life, we have no choice in the matter; they will come. And usually, when we are not prepared for them. Although we can't choose when our difficult days arise, we can choose how we react to them.

Life has taught me perseverance, but this job has taught me the strength in understanding. There are so many people who deal with problems every day. And many have yet to learn the important coping skills that will help them make smart decisions and move forward. When a child calls you a name or misbehaves, is it personal? Or is he/she just being a child? In the same way, we have adults who have stunted their mental growth with drugs, alcohol, or other vices. Children run on emotion. Adults are expected to experience the emotion – good or bad – without pushing it away or reacting to that emotion before they have time to process it. I see too many adults who lack this skill. They behave like impulsive children.

Thank you for reading. I understand that some of what's shared here may have been difficult to take in. These incidents happen every day across the country, and the men and women on the front lines carry them long after their shifts end – often replaying them in their minds when they return home to their families. Yet they continue to show up, standing between others and experiencing what no one should have to endure.

It's important to understand what is happening around us, even when it's uncomfortable. To understand what first responders face – and what so many individuals quietly struggle with each day.

Because understanding leads to compassion, and compassion creates space for forgiveness. And in a world that often feels divided, those may be the most powerful forces we have.

And still, we move forward.

ACKNOWLEDGMENTS

I would like to thank Life Sized Publishing for giving me the opportunity to share my story. They never once rushed me or set a deadline, and they always gave good suggestions without telling me it had to be written their way. I want to thank my editor, Karen, for braving a tornado to work on this project, and all the time she put in. I also want to thank Justin for reaching out to me and being the catalyst for getting this started. This book would still just be another file sitting on a thumb drive without these people.

I want to thank my family and friends for always encouraging me. My close friends for partaking in some of these stories. And my wife and step-son for always asking me what I'm working on.

Lastly, I want to thank my department for giving me the chance. My coworkers who have become friends, and my coworkers who have my back.

Recommended Reading

Books I highly recommend everyone to read regarding physical and mental health:

The Plant Paradox and The Energy Paradox by Steven M. Gundry, M.D. – *The Plant Paradox* compiles so much information on the "healthy foods" that are causing us damage due to large sticky proteins called Lectins. Dr. Gundry goes into detail on the process of how a lot of our foods are made and labeled. The Energy Paradox is a great read for anyone looking to understand why we can be so fatigued with having an excess of different foods and energy products. Dr. Gundry describes the cycles that our bodies go through with not only sleep but also with eating, highlighting the importance of fasting.

Brain Saver by Anthony William is a wonderfully exhaustive book on the foods and products that are affecting our physical and mental health and how our brain acts as a second filter for wastes. William lists every mental and physical health condition and highlights the importance of eliminating toxic metal contaminants from the brain.

Brain Energy by Christopher M. Palmer, M.D. – *Brain Energy* highlights the importance of what we eat and when we eat it. The book highlights the importance of the mitochondria of every cell and their function to produce energy for us as a whole. Dr. Palmer taps into territory that is new in the study of brain health by describing in depth how metals get trapped and collected in our brain tissue and cause every type of major issue. The end of the book is filled with recipes for whole food detoxes that I highly recommend.

Psycho-Cybernetics by Maxwell Maltz, M.D. – An oldie but a goody. This was my first book that opened the door to my understanding of willpower and drive, and how the mind really is the driving force behind our lives. I'm not one to advocate for self-help books as I believe that life is the greatest teacher, but this is a good reminder of just how powerful our minds can be.

How Not To Die by Michael Greger, M.D. – Dr. Gregor is a huge advocate for a vegan diet and explains why in his book. I always use caution when mentioning to people that I try to stick to a vegan diet. My self-control is awful on my days off as I eat whatever I want. And it's important to make sure you're getting the proper vitamins and minerals when restricting your diet. Unfortunately, some strict vegans have gotten sick by limiting themselves. I would highly recommend checking out Dr. Greger's online resource Nu tritionfacts.org first, where you can find a plethora of great articles on his work.

Breath by James Nestor – If I had to describe the whole premise of the book in one sentence, it would be "close your mouth and breathe through your nose." Nester does an amazing job highlighting the importance of breathing through our nose, especially during sleep. He goes in-depth into health issues associated with breathing the wrong way and also describes how it's possible to control our health, immune system, and temperature with the right breathing techniques.

Thinking Fast and Slow by Daniel Kahneman – A difficult read unless you really enjoy understanding how our brains function and solve problems efficiently. Kahneman talks about the two systems of the brain and how they differ.

ABOUT THE AUTHOR

Alan Merrick was born in Central New York where he currently resides with his family. He studied Human Services and Psychology after high school and started work at the Rescue Mission in the homeless shelter and drug and alcohol rehabilitation program. After working there for several years he started his career in law enforcement with his local police department where he currently serves on midnight patrol. He is a veteran of his police department of ten years and is a new author of fiction and non-fiction. Besides writing in his free time, he enjoys spending time with his family and cooking. Alan currently still volunteers at the Rescue Mission where he worked by speaking in the chapel service once a month.

His goal is to reach people through his writing and eventually publish more books that he hopes will inspire and educate, if at the very least stories that people will enjoy.